Rabbit and Me

All you need to know about your pet rabbit

By Emi Lau

Copyright©2015

Disclaimer: The information and advice contained in this book is for educational reference only and should not be considered as a substitute for professional veterinary medical advice. You should seek professional veterinary advice regarding all health and wellness matters.

Table of Contents

Just one second...

You can download free contents at

www.AnimalWhoop.com/RabbitAndMe

You will be getting the following for free:

- A health checklist that you can print and keep in your pocket when you go to look for your ideal rabbit
- A step-by-step guide on how to make your own rabbit toys

Thank you for your support. Please leave a review on Amazon so that we can improve our books.

Introduction

When researching on how to take care of my two rabbits, I found information difficult to come across and often very confusing. This book is aimed to help others who experienced the same problems as I did when looking for pet care advice. Here, I have written pet care information based on my own experiences and research in the hopes that anyone who needs help with their rabbits will find what they need.

In this book, you will learn about:

- Should you get a pet rabbit
- How to choose a healthy rabbit
- Different rabbit breeds
- How to keep an indoor rabbit
- The equipment you need
- How to litter train your rabbit
- How to bunny proof your house
- Bonding with your rabbits and make them like you
- Should you neuter your rabbit
- Nail clipping
- How to prevent your rabbit getting heat stroke

You can also get some free downloads that come with this book by going on our website www.AnimalWhoop.com/RabbitAndMe. The free downloads include the health checklist that you can print and keep in your pocket when you go to look for your ideal rabbit, also a step-by-step guide on how to make your own rabbit toys.

History of rabbits

Today's pet shop rabbit derives from the European rabbit. While there are several different species of rabbits, such as swamp rabbits, cottontail rabbits etc. The European rabbit is the only one to be domesticated. All those colourful breeds came from the European. Hard to imagine how that could happen when you consider patterns in breeds like the Dutch.

Rabbits began life in this world as wild and free but very soon, when Romans discovered them, they were captured and kept as a source of meat. At first rabbits were able to dig themselves out of these Roman pens but soon after, fenced warrens were made to contain them. It was also the Romans who introduced the European rabbit to the United Kingdom. Those wild rabbits you see in the fields were the work of the Romans.

The domestication of the rabbit did not occur till a bit later in the middle ages. French monks were responsible for this as they searched for a meat they can keep within the monastery. New-born rabbits were not considered as meat so were fine to eat during lent. It wasn't long before rabbits were being bred by the monks for certain traits and colours, this was the beginning of selective breeding for rabbits. There were some suggestions that some of the richer ladies during this period had kept rabbits for colours and traits.

Then in come the Victorians who started breeding some of the fancier breeds of rabbits available. Since rabbits were easy to keep in towns and cities, they soon became more than a source of meat and were considered pets for children and families.

Interestingly, rabbits were kept in people's gardens during the World Wars in both US and UK where people were encourage to keep them for their meat and for their fur to make clothes. After the war, more people had rabbits for pets. With even more breeds being developed all over the world, rabbits were increasing in popularity for both families and rabbit fanciers.

Today, rabbits are the third most popular pet.

The relationship between rabbits and human

What are rabbits to many people? They are beloved pets and companions. They are the third most popular pet with their popularity on the rise. Rabbits now have a very special relationship with many humans. With more people being educated on the needs of a pet rabbit and more people owning house rabbits, the lives of domesticated rabbits have never been better. Their inquisitive and stubborn nature makes them interesting pets with great personality and while looking after rabbits requires a lot of time, money and effort, it is worth every second.

They do make dangerous pets if a non-neutered male and female are placed together. Due to their fast reproductive rates and large litter sizes, backyard breeding can occur quite often, sometimes accidentally when pet shops have not ascertained the gender of the rabbits. Even with experience, it can be difficult to figure out the gender of a young rabbit.

While they do make great pets for both the old and the young, they are not for everybody. This book will help you find out whether rabbits are suitable for you.

Chapter 1: Should I get a rabbit

Rabbits are very rewarding pets but they require a lot of work. Many rabbits end up being rehomed due to people not understanding the needs of their pet. This chapter is written in the hopes that it may aid you in deciding if a rabbit is the right pet for you.

These are a few of the things you should consider before choosing to own a bunny:

Will you have the time and energy to look after a rabbit?

Rabbits are energetic animals. To put one in a hutch all day is considered cruel. Like dogs, they require every day exercise and if you are unable to meet that requirement daily, rabbits may not be the pet for you. Wild rabbits can run as much as 30-40 tennis courts per day and domesticated rabbits should be given a decent amount of 'out of cage/hutch' time per day. Without regular exercise and play, rabbits can become bored, overweight and develop physical and emotion problems.

Is this a pet for a child?

Rabbits are fragile and do not like being picked up. Like cats, rabbits will choose when they want your attention, you should not force a rabbit to play or cuddle an unwilling rabbit as this can cause stress and the rabbit may nip or kick. This means they are not ideal for young children. Rabbits can make ideal pets for older children but ultimately parents and caretakers will be responsible for the rabbit. Rabbits need daily care (feeding, changing water, spot cleaning living quarters and daily play). Having said that, keeping rabbits is a good way to teach responsibility to a child as long as parents and caretakers understand that they should supervise a young

11

child with a rabbit and that if the child ever becomes disinterested, it is the parent's responsibility to ensure the rabbit's needs are met. Bear in mind, rabbits can live as long as ten years.

If you do want a family rabbit, larger breeds are recommended as they have calmer temperaments. Young children will have trouble picking larger rabbits up so will be less likely to injure them or be injured. Bigger rabbits are also sturdier.

Rabbits may be cheap to buy but are not cheap to keep

The cost of a hutch or cage can be as expensive as £100. With a bit of shopping around on the internet you may find decent size cages from £40 but the larger your rabbit the larger the living space must be.

Rule of thumb is to buy the biggest possible cage or hutch you can afford without limiting the rabbits movements. A rabbit should be able to hop three times from one side to the other and should be able to stand up fully without touching the top of their home. If you intend to have an outdoor rabbit, a run will be necessary to provide exercise space.

Rabbit equipment such as water bottles, food bowls, hay racks, beds and litter trays will add to the cost.

Neutering is another expense to consider.

These are one-time expenses and if you choose carefully, they can last for years.

Monthly expenses will be rabbit food, hay (you will need quite a bit of this), litter and bedding.

Yearly expenses will include vaccinations.

Expenses you cannot predict will be vet bills and as these can cost a lot, insurance is recommended.

In conclusion, the start-up costs of owning a rabbit can be quite large. Once everything is established, monthly expenses will not be very large and if you have insurance you will not have to worry about sudden vet bills.

Will you have an indoor rabbit or an outdoor rabbit?

It is a good idea to consider how you will house a rabbit. If you house your rabbit inside, there are many housing options to choose from, such as cages or DIY rabbit houses using wire square cubes. You will also need to rabbit proof the rooms and areas you intend to allow your rabbit to roam.

Indoor rabbits can develop close bonds with humans but they may scratch and bite furniture and flooring. Rabbit proofing a home is an on-going process as rabbits will think of new ways to do naughty things. House rabbits can be very rewarding as they might sit on your lap in the evenings when you read or watch TV, they might follow you around the house and you will be able to witness some rabbit behaviours you may miss if they were outdoors.

If you house your rabbit in your garden, you will need to think about getting a hutch or a shed and a run for exercise. Outdoor rabbits might get lonely on their own and if you let your rabbit on your lawn you will have to be prepared for rabbits to eat and potentially ruin it. It is also important to identify any poisonous plants in your garden.

How many rabbits are you thinking of getting?

Rabbits are social animals, that means that they do not like being alone. Most breeders or rabbit rescuers recommend a pair and some rescuers only let you adopt their rabbits if you take in a bonded pair.

A bonded pair is strongly recommended for several reasons.

- Being with another rabbit affects a rabbit's emotional wellbeing positively and can reduce stress.
- Female and male pairs can fall in love which is a joy to witness (please ensure both are spayed and neutered to avoid many baby buns!)
- Rabbits will groom each other often so if one of your rabbits is prone to getting dirt in the corner of their eyes, their partner will help them out.
- If you are out for most of the day a pair will keep each other company.

I also recommend that you choose to get a pair of rabbits if you decide to house them outside as one will be quite lonely.

It is also recommended that if you choose to keep a pair you should try to find a female and male rabbit. The reason for this is that the chances of a same sex pair bonding are lower than two different sex rabbits. If you choose a male/male or a female/female bonding, they may be alright together when young but once they hit a certain age they may end up fighting. If this concerns you, it is best to find a female/male pair.

Consider the other pets you currently own

Do you want to pair a rabbit with a guinea pig? Whilst in some scenarios guinea pigs and rabbits are able to co-exist, it is not recommended to house them together.

Buying a rabbit to add to a guinea pig's cage is not a good idea as rabbits often binky when happy or jump around a lot. Their hind legs have a lot of power and even if they unintentionally kick your piggy it can result in serious injury. There is also the issue of one possibly bullying the other or hogging the food. Both are completely different species and do not communicate with each other so being together does not offer either any benefits.

If you have a cat you will need to be aware that a cat can be a threat to small bunnies. They may be treated like prey so a larger breed will be more suitable. Cats can live in a house with a rabbit very well in some cases. In other cases rabbits have been known to bully cats!

If you own a dog you must never leave your rabbit in the same room as your dog unsupervised. Even if your dog is trained there is still a small chance that it might revert to its instincts to hunt. Extra care must be taken if introducing a rabbit and dog.

Looking for a rabbit to go with your current rabbit? Bonding two rabbits in a difficult task but where done successfully could lead to happier bunnies.

Exotic animals like ferrets, birds and reptiles should not be kept within close proximity to a rabbit. Ferrets and some reptiles consider rabbits to be quite tasty and ferrets can be extremely clever so unless you want them to have your rabbit for lunch then you best keep them apart. Birds that hunt will scare your rabbit when they screech and that will stress them out. In some cases small birds have gotten on well with rabbits but it is quite rare to see it happen.

Buying a rabbit: Young or old?

Whether you choose an old rabbit or a young rabbit is really personal preference. There are some advantages and disadvantages to both though.

Young rabbits are often cuter but at the same time they are more energetic and require more care. They can be more destructive, although this is not always the case.

Mature rabbits are usually available through adoption and they have their own perks.

Older rabbits are usually more calm and littered trained. Older rabbits (and some young ones) usually come from rescue centres. You will have a better understanding of the rabbit's personality. Depending on which rescue centre you go to, the rabbit may be vaccinated, chipped or neutered/spayed. That can save you some money and if you are looking for a pair, some rescue centres can help you look for a bonded pair that gets on well.

Should I get the rabbit from breeder of pet shop?

Rabbits can be purchased from breeders or pet shops and they can also be adopted from rescue centres:

Breeders

Breeders tend to be more reputable, are able to provide you with more accurate information and if you are after a certain breed, it is a good idea to visit a breeder. When I say breeder, I do not mean casual breeders who breed for profit or those who choose irresponsibly to not neutering/spaying their pets. I mean professional breeders such as show rabbit breeders. Professional breeders should be able to tell you the parents and grandparents of their rabbits, possible health issues and will let you see the parents with the litter. Their rabbits are usually used to being handled so should be less likely to have personality problems.

Rescue centres

Rescue centres are good places to choose a pet from. There is a large variety of rabbits, from young to old, from Dutch to Belgian hare. Centres will also offer you lots of information and support as the permanent rehoming of a rabbit is what they aim for so to them it is important to do everything properly.

Many rabbits are abandoned and unwanted every year and they are all looking for a good home. A good site is Rabbit Rehome (www.rabbitrehome.org.uk). Here you can search for rabbits to adopt by breed, size, age, sex, and whether it is vaccinated or neutered or bonded. Bear in mind that any vaccinated rabbit will need to have booster vaccinations every 6 months for myxomatosis and a booster once a year for VHD. Many vets are now offering a once a year combo booster so call up your local vet to see what they offer and the prices.

Pet shops

Pet shops are hit and miss in general. You may be lucky and purchase a decent pet with no health problems but you might also be very unlucky like I was when I purchased my two rabbits where there were health issues and where they were sexed wrong.

Pet shops are generally places where people are trying to make money and they may not be the most informed when it comes to buying a pet. It is hard to identify the gender of a young rabbit and if they get it wrong you may be getting more than you bargained for. Some rabbits are more prone to teeth and eye health problems and pet shops will be less likely to identify and inform you of these problems. In these respects and also in terms of information for rabbit care, pet shops are not as good as breeders or rescue centres.

My rabbits having a goooood time

Chapter 2: Choosing your pet rabbit

Buying any pet is an important process and you really need to take care when choosing a pet. It should never be an impulse buy and you should always have all the necessary housing and equipment set up at home. It is important to choose a healthy animal as you do not want to be faced with vet bills within the first week.

It is also important not to choose an animal because you feel sorry for it for reasons such as the animal being ill or being the runt of the pack. This may lead to heartbreak, possible behavioural problems and increased vet bills.

Never be afraid to ask questions and always make sure you understand the answers.

Research is really important, backyard breeders and some pet shops will not know a lot about the animal they are selling you. So make it a point to know your animal before you buy it.

Chapter 2.1: How to choose a healthy pet rabbit

The steps below will help you in the process of choosing the right rabbit.

1.   **Check your surroundings, is the place clean?** The cage where the rabbit is kept should not be excessively dirty. Droppings are understandable but it needs to look like it has been cleaned regularly. Droppings should also be hard dry circular balls (rather like the cereal coco pops), if the droppings are soft then the health of the rabbits in the cage may not be very good.

2.   **How old are the animals?** Rabbits are reliant on their mother for the first few weeks of their lives so they should not be separated from their mother until they are weaned. A rabbit should stay with the mother till it is at least 10 weeks old. If the place you are considering buying from has rabbits younger than this then you really should not buy them and inform them that their pets are too young.

3.   **Is the rabbit active?** While you would not expect older rabbits to be jumping around, with young rabbits you should expect some movement and curiosity. A rabbit lying down and looking disinterested in its surroundings could have an underlying problem. It is normal for rabbits to be a bit shy or nervous as they are prey animals but if they have been handled properly they should not be afraid or scared.

Bear in mind that rabbits are more active at certain times of the day. E.g. they are usually most active during early morning and late evening. It is also a good idea to check if the rabbit you are interested in has any problems with movement.

4. **Are the rabbits sneezing a lot or scratching a lot?** Rabbits do not often get infected by fleas but it can still happen and sneezing may be a sign of nose problems or an illness like snuffles. You should always handle the animal you are interested in; this enables you to check its health and to see its personality. A well socialised rabbit should not bite aggressively. If the breeder or pet shop does not let you do that then you should find somewhere more reputable. When handling the rabbit you should always check the following:

Are the eyes, nose, ears and mouth clean? Eyes should be bright and alert, they should not be watering or have gunk in the corners. Nose should be mostly dry and pink. It should not be dirty. Ears should also be clean with no signs of parasites or injuries. You should check the teeth. Some breeds are more susceptible to teeth conditions where teeth may not meet perfectly (malocclusion) and this can vary in severity but in worst cases it can cause problems for the rabbit to eat. A reputable breeder will inform you of any teeth issues but best to have a look yourself.

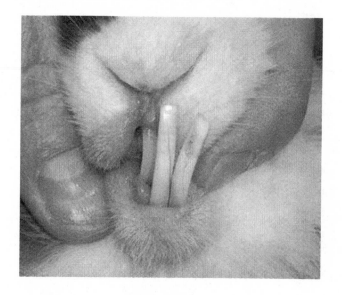

(Pic 1, Bradygnathia superior in a rabbit By Uwe Gille)

Is the fur clean and shiny? Rabbits groom a lot, in fact they groom as much as cats do and in a healthy rabbit the coat should look good and feel soft. There should be no bald spots or injuries. Check that the feet are not sore (this can happen if they are left to stand on wired flooring for too long). The tail should have fur and the area around the anus and genitals should be clean. There should be no faeces stuck to the bottom as this means the rabbit has diarrhea. There should also be no signs of flystrike, a condition where flies lay eggs onto the bottom of a rabbit and the larvae eat the rabbit's flesh.

The rabbit should not smell bad. The area it uses as a toilet may smell slightly but overall it should not be over powering and the fur of the rabbit should not smell strongly of anything.

5.   Ask about the parentage of the rabbit and whether there is a history of illnesses in the parents and grandparents. If you are buying from a breeder they should be able to offer you answers to these questions, at least for parents of the rabbit. Where possible ask to see the parents to get a good idea of size of your rabbit.

Download the free health short checklist at
www.AnimalWhoop.com/RabbitAndMe. You can print and
keep in your pocket when you go to look for your ideal rabbit:

Chapter 2.2: Different breeds of rabbits

You may have seen rabbits in all different colours and sizes. Even though all domesticated rabbits came from the European rabbit, different rabbit breeds are available. As they can vary in needs and temperaments, here is a brief description of some of the common breeds.

The breeds included here are not recognised by all rabbit associations, thus are not eligible breeds for showing, depending on your location.

The max weights mentioned are there for reference only. These are max weights for show animals and rabbits bred for pets may not necessarily follow those maximums.

Dwarf Rabbit Breeds

This category of rabbits is the one that you would have probably seen on birthday cards or calendars. They are not all recognised as 'breeds' but they are popular little rabbits.

When buying a dwarf rabbit, one must be careful as there have been cases where pet shops do not know the parents of their bunnies and the 'dwarf rabbit' turns out to have mixed parents, and can grow to a large size.

Dwarf breeds are considered to be under 1.81kg and most of them carry a dwarfing gene with the exception of the Britannia Petite.

Examples of Dwarf Rabbits:

American Fuzzy Lop - max 1.60 kg

(Pic 2: American Fuzzy Lop rabbit. White buck)

Recognised by ARBA, this is a dwarf breed that has a wool

similar to angora. They are fluffy small rabbits with a sociable nature. They enjoy attention and work well with people and other rabbits.

Britannia Petite - max 1.20 kg

(Pic 3: Roodoog Pool by Gilberte)

This breed of rabbit is one of the lightest in the category. They make poor pets for children as without proper handling, they are more likely to nip. With patience, these very active rabbits can be decent pets. However, they are less forgiving if you do not use a positive approach to training them. Britannia Petites are extremely active and require plenty of room for exercise.

Holland Lop/Miniature Lop - max 1.81/1.60 kg

(Pic 4: by valeehill via Flickr)

Depending on which association you look at, this rabbit has two names. ARBA call it the Holland Lop and BRC refer to this breed as a Miniature Lop. There are also fundamental differences in the rules both associations have for showing these rabbits, based on factors like maximum weight, poses etc. Aside from these and despite two different names, they are essentially the same thing. This lop has a short round face and a rounded body. It has a good temperament and can be very cuddly.

Jersey Wooly - max 1.578 kg

(Pic 5: by_hiwarz_ via Flickr)

Bunnies of this breed have an easy to care for wooly coat. They are playful and friendly rabbits.

Lionhead Rabbit - max 1.70 kg

(Pic 6: by coalybunny via Flickr)

This breed is not recognised by the ARBA however, the BRC do see it as a legit breed. They have a mane of hair around their head which explains their name. These rabbits can have both lop and upright ears. They are generally friendly and calm rabbits. Easily tame, they are able to learn basic commands.

Netherland Dwarf - max 1.134 kg

(Pic 7: Netherland Dwarf By Lauri Rantala)

Most dwarf breeds owe their thanks to the dwarfing gene that is found in the Netherland Dwarf. However, this gene can be lethal if two true dwarf rabbits are bred, leading to a small percentage of their litter dying. To reduce these kinds of deaths, breeders tend to mix true dwarfs with false dwarf. Small wild rabbits played a big part in the breeding of the Netherland Dwarf so some rabbits of this breed can be a bit nervous or 'wild' compared to other breeds. However, with selective breeding, most Netherland Dwarfs make good pets and are quite docile. They are small but strong.

Small Rabbit Breeds

Small breeds are heavier and bigger than dwarf rabbits. They tend not to get heavier than 3.2kg. They make better pets for young children as they are not too much bigger than a dwarf yet they are hardier and less likely to nip.

Dutch - max 2.26 kg

This is a beautiful rabbit with very distinctive markings. Dutch rabbits make popular and are caring mothers. Because of this caring nature, Dutches have been used as foster mothers in certain situations.

Most dutches have white fur with coloured patches over the eyes, cheeks and ears. This leaves an upside down 'V' of white on their forehead. They then have a large block of colour starting midback and ending at the feet, leaving them with white socks.

Dutches have a variety of colours, with black & white, blue & white and brown & white being seen more often in pet shops. There is something called a tri-coloured Dutch which has three colours instead of the two colour pairing seen in most Dutches.

English Angora - max 3.402 kg

(Pic 8: by Squish_E via Flickr)

The Angora rabbit requires a lot of grooming and care due to the wooly fur that covers its entire body. This gives the rabbit an appearance of a ball of fluff. This wool can be used in the making of garments and can be cut off as when the rabbit is moulting. The English Angora is not suitable for young children because of the level of care that is required in keeping this rabbit. There are other types of Angora but the English one has a unique facial features in that it is the only one to have wool all over the eyes. They are laid back gentle rabbits who enjoy company.

Havana - max 2.72 kg

(Pic 9: Havana Rabbit breed By Mjm91)

These rabbits are famous for their high luster fur and are known as the 'mink' of the rabbit family. Havanas have short bodies and legs. They do not look particularly special to pet owners as they tend to have one colour.

Mini Lop - max 2.38 kg

(Pic 10: by _katattack via Flickr)

Mini lop is also known as the Dwarf Lop in UK. Despite the name, it is not a dwarf breed. This sturdy lop eared rabbit is a good rabbit for children and is not too large. They are an intelligent breed and can learn commands. These friendly rabbits are not afraid of showing you their disapproval if you do not give them enough attention.

Mini Rex - max 2 kg

(Pic 11: by Carly & Art via Flickr)

The Mini Rex is a smaller version of the Rex. This breed is famous for its soft velvet coat which is the result of a mutation that causes guard hairs to be as short as the undercoat. The Mini Rex comes in a huge variety of colours.

Silver - max 2.72 kg

(Pic 12: Schwarzes Kleinsilber-Kaninchen By 4028mdk09)

One of the older breeds, the Silver has longer ears and a longer body. The name comes from the silver white coloured hairs scattered across the coat, known as ticking. The Silver rabbit has become increasingly rare with less than 100 annual registrations in the USA.

Standard Chinchilla - max 3.1 kg

(Pic 13: House rabbit, Standard Chinchilla breed by Xoxi)

As the name implies, the Chinchilla rabbit has beautiful fur which was the result of Himalayan/Beveren/Wild Rabbit pairings. This breed is known for being gentle and energetic at the same time making them ideal for kids. The Chinchilla breed is most often used for showing or for the fur.

Tan - max 2.041 kg

(Pic 14: A Tan rabbit (black) owned by Kelly Flynn of Blue Ribbon Rabbitry By Kelly Flynn – Blue Ribbon Rabbitry)

A friendly rabbit that is known for reddish brown marks on the feet, ears, belly and face. It is a thin and longer looking breed. Interestingly enough, ARBA allows Tan rabbits to move around freely when being judged whereas other rabbits are supposed to keep still. They are not lap or cuddly bunnies but are extremely active and can be trained to complete in rabbit agility courses.

Medium Rabbit Breeds

Being larger, these rabbits also require more space. If you are thinking of having house rabbits and you are limited in space, be aware that medium breeds and larger need bigger cages. In some cases, using puppy play pens or even crates are better and cheaper options for housing a medium sized rabbit. It also follows that if the rabbit is to live in the garden, the hutch should be larger. They would require more food but are generally considered more outgoing and tolerant of handling although this varies from breed to breed.

American Sable - max 4.5 kg

(Pic 15: American Sable Rabbit By Sonofsammie)

The American Sable came from crossing Chinchilla rabbits. They have a particular fur colouring that is quite like a siamese cat: whilst the main body colour is a light beige, the head, tail, ears and feet are a darker brown. Eyes tend to be slightly red. A peaceful and friendly breed that may spend most of the day resting, the American Sable can be a good companion to either a human or another rabbit.

Belgian Hare - max 2.08 kg

(Pic 16: Hasenkaninchen By Hagen Graebner)

Whilst the Belgian Hare looks like a hare, it is basically a rabbit that looks more racey. This is an old breed with an arched body shape and deep red fur. In America, this breed is considered hard to breed properly and tends not be very popular as a pet. However, the shape and appearance of this rabbit makes it a unique one to choose.

Blanc de Hotot - max 4.98 kg

(Pic 17: Her head tilt is much improved today, but not quite back to normal. Hotot Rabbit By Carly & Art)

Similar to the Dwarf Hotot, this is the medium sized version. There was once a Giant Hotot but that breed has now become extinct. The body is completely white apart from a ring of black around the eyes, a bit like eye liner.

Californian - max 4.5 kg

(Pic 18: Russenkaninchen By Lisa Göris)

Created by crossing the Himalayan, Chinchilla and New Zealand Whites, this rabbit has a white body and black ears, nose, feet and tail. The breed was made with the intention of becoming a meat rabbit with a good pelt. Their good temperament makes them ideal for children.

English Spot - max 3.62 kg

(Pic 19: A young English Spot rabbit By Kat Chzhen)

An interesting looking breed, this rabbit has a distinct patterning. English Spots have a white base fur with a coloured (there are several colours but common is black) line down the centre of the back, a butterfly marking on the nose, lined eyes and a series of spots that go across the sides. As it is a full arched rabbit, they are allowed to move when being judged at a show. They are active rabbits that enjoy jumping around but can be nervous.

French Angora - max 4.76 kg

(Pic 20: By Loggie-log)

The French Angora has fur that can be harvested for wool. This rabbit has no wool on its face, front feet and ears. Grooming is an important part of looking after an angora rabbit which means this breed is only suitable for those who are willing to brush them every day. However, this pays off as you can learn to harvest and use the wool of your rabbit. French Angoras come in many colours.

Giant Angora - max 4.5 kg

(Pic 21: Joey, Giant Angora Rabbit Buck By Oldhaus)

With white fur and ruby eyes, the Giant Angora produces the most wool due to a dense undercoat. Most of its body is covered in wool. Like other angoras, grooming is necessary every day. This larger angora breed takes a year or more to mature fully.

Harlequin - max 3.62 kg

(Pic 22: LAPIN JAPONAIS, public domain)

Brightly coloured, to the untrained eye, the Harlequin's patterns look random. Some people believe Harlequin to be a fur colour rather than a breed, however, it is recognised by both BRC and ARBA. The common colours is black and orange and the main aim is to have half the face one colour and the other half the second colour. The rest of the body should be half-half in colour too. This is a friendly breed that is both playful and gentle.

Palomino - max 4.5 kg

(Pic 23: Golden Palomino Buck by Jamaltby)

This rabbit has large upright ears and brown eyes with fur colour being either a golden or a lynx colour. Palomino rabbits were bred using a variety of breeds including meat rabbits as the aim was to create a meaty rabbit with a nice appearance.

Rex - max 3.62 kg

This is the bigger version of the Mini Rex. It should be noted that the max weight here follows BRC standards. The ARBA standards ask for a heavier rabbit. The Rex has a fine silky textured fur that comes in many colours and patterns. Due to their fur having guard hairs the same length as the undercoat, their fur demands less grooming. In terms of personality, it is often reported that Rexs are friendly maternal rabbits that enjoy company.

Rhinelander - max 4.5 kg

(Pic 25: Simon the Rhinelander By Rabbit Mage)

An arched breed, this rabbit is known for its white background with black and orange butterfly markings. ARBA also accepts blue and fawn spotting. They are not an aggressive breed and are laid back in nature. The Rhinelander is allowed to pose and run as it likes when being judged as it is an arched breed.

Satin - max 3.62 kg

(Pic 26: Satin blau By Blauglanz)

As you may have already guessed, the Satin rabbit has a satin like fur. They are larger in the US as they are regarded as a meat breed over there whereas in UK the Satin is a fur breed. Satin rabbits have a gene mutation that causes the guard hairs to become transparent and reflect light to create that satin sheen.

Satin Angora - max 4.30 kg

(Pic 27: Satin angora rabbit By Clevername)

An Angora breed with finer fur, the Satin Angora is covered in angora fur all over apart from on the ears and the head. The fur has a shiny sheen to it. Like all Angoras, this breed would need special grooming and diet.

Chapter 3: Indoor rabbit housing

Keeping rabbits inside the home is becoming increasingly popular and due to the amount of time a rabbit gets to spend with its owners indoors, a deep bond can form between them. Because of this, it is sometimes acceptable to keep one rabbit as long as the owner spends enough time playing with the bunny that it won't feel lonely.

Cages are the main method and the easiest to get hold off. ⁺ net stores with the space sell them and they are quite accessible online. A cage consists of a deep plastic tray with a wire top. Shop around and you will see that most cages come as a set, with a water bottle, food bowl, hay rack and a platform/hiding hole for the rabbit. Look at the points below to learn more about cages.

- Most cages are at a length of 100-120cm; this is fine for a rabbit that will be spending most of its time out of the cage. Ideally, you should choose the largest one you are able to afford. While some manufacturers try to sell cages smaller than 100cm as dwarf rabbit cages, please do not use them! Anything smaller than 100cm is definitely too small.
If you are buying a young rabbit, always choose a cage for its adult size.
If your rabbit will be confined in a cage during your sleeping hours and your work hours, I would recommend you to find a cage that was 120+cm in size.
If you will be rabbit proofing the room the cage will be in (or the entire house) and you are considering letting your rabbit roam free throughout the whole day, a 100cm cage will suffice.

- Rabbit cages have a door to allow you access to the pet. Some have more than one door for ease of access and size of doors can vary greatly. While it does not seem like an important point to consider, think about a scenario where a door may be too small for you to spot clean with ease or to remove a litter tray. Some doors are more suited to guinea pigs than rabbits!

- Some cages come with metal wire flooring. These can damage a rabbit's hands and feet so the flooring will have to be covered. This applies to wire doors that form ramps when opened.

- Like hutches, you can now buy two storey cages. But do not forget that the need for a ramp will mean areas of the cage are not usable.

There are many methods to keep your rabbits rather than just using cages. We will go through some of the most popular one in this chapter.

- Cages
- Club Houses
- Dog Exercise Pens
- Dog Crates
- Free Ranged

Cages are rather like bedrooms for rabbits

You sleep in your room but you would not want to be confined to just your room. Adequate time out of a cage to exercise is a must. This applies to any other indoor housing method where the home itself is not very roomy. I would recommend the use of a cage if you are able to let your rabbit out to exercise often. They can be relatively inexpensive (but expensive for the amount of size you get) if you shop around on the internet and because most come with accessories, you do not need to buy those separately. They are also easy to set up; you can have a cage all ready in less than half an hour. Aside from bunny proofing your rabbits play area, there are fewer changes to make to your house and less DIY/creativity work needed.

When finding a place to put the cage, it would be better to place it in a room rather than a hallway. This is because hallways have a lot more draughts and can be quite busy noisy areas. Since cages and most indoor housing methods involve metal wire frames, they are vulnerable to draughts so careful thought into placement of these rabbit homes is needed. Rabbits are quite shy when in a new home so to put the cage in a hallway may frighten a rabbit and if your household is noisy, it might prevent your rabbit from relaxing.

(Let me out!)

Cube Houses (For advanced rabbit owners)

This is one of the most creative and fun ideas I have seen. It is extremely versatile, you will have the freedom to make your rabbit house exactly how you want it and if you want a change in scenery, you can always take it apart and start again. They are made from storage cubes called Neat Idea Cubes (sold by Fellowes) that were meant to be an alternative to other storage methods. You can combine several packs of these wire frames to make a quite large cage. They usually come in packs of 20 frames with connectors (you can also use cable ties).

You can add shelves and doors where you want and extensions if you feel like it. You will need wood to support any shelves you add and as rabbits do not do well standing on wire frames, you will need to place lino, carpet or wooden board on top of the shelves as lining. Doors can be secured with binder clips. Trays can be made from wood and lined with lino or made from corrugated plastic that can be scored and folded into a tray.

One disadvantage of making these in UK is that you may have trouble finding all the necessary equipment since these cubes are not as popular here. It can be just as expensive (maybe more expensive) than buying a cage, as these cubes are more expensive here in the UK than in the USA. It also requires time to build. A main advantage is that you are able to build a cage to suit your bunny's needs, it can be big, have several levels, be made to a certain design to make the most of the area you have. For example, if you have an area of the room available that is 'L' shaped, a normal cage would not have allowed you to make the most efficient use of that area but with these wire frames, you can build an 'L' shape cage.

Like cages, be sure to think carefully about where to position a cube house as it is very susceptible to drought.

Exercise Pens and Dog Crates

This method of housing involves using a premade pen or crate and then renovating it to suit your needs. It is ideal for those who want some customisation similar to what cube houses has but has neither the time nor skill to build from scratch. Customisation can be as simple as laying down a bed and toys or as complex to adding shelves.

An exercise pen is a bit like a run but suitable for indoor use. If your rabbit is able to ace that jump, cover the top with cloth. An old bed sheet will do, this would put them off trying to jump out. There are also taller exercise pens available. You can buy exercise pens online. They are quite convenient in that they allow you to move the panels in a way that will fit in the room that you have. Exercise pens can give you a lot of space without costing you the amount a cage might. Most pens come with a door that you can open and let your bunny out to exercise. While using a pen as housing gives you plenty of space, your bunny will still need to be allowed out to play. Here are some pointers for exercise pens:

- Lining the floor with lino will protect your carpet and makes any spills easy to clean.

- Provide a place for your bunny to hide should they become scared.
- Cardboard boxes are cheap second levels and hiding holes. Your rabbit can jump on them to look around, can hide when scared and can dig or chew it for fun. Just replace when necessary.
- Cat boxes make more permanent second levels and hiding holes.
- Ramps can be made to reach second levels.

If you do not intend to move the pen often, with a bit of DIY, you can use sheets of corrugated plastic or boards of wood to create a 'wall' to line the walls of the pen. It doesn't need to be very high, just high enough to stop stray bits of hay and litter falling out will make for a neater home.

As a form of housing, I believe that an exercise pen is the quickest and possibly cheapest set up. You do not need to have a high level of DIY skill and if you ever need to move the pen or even move houses, the pen folds up. Your rabbit will get a lot more space to roam and if you have more than one rabbit, the extra space will mean they are less likely to fight. Cleaning is easy as you can literally step into the pen whereas using a cage, cube house or dog crate will require crawling into small spaces to grab things like litter trays. The biggest disadvantage of using an exercise pen is that it is not predator proof. To prevent cats jumping in, a cover for the top will do the trick. However the spacing between the bars in a pen is large enough for a paw to get in. If you have a cat that is likely to see your rabbit as a meal, you should consider searching for a pen with smaller spacing and providing several hiding holes so your rabbit can hide if it feels threatened.

Dog crates for rabbits

Dog crates were made to keep dogs confined within the house. It's primarily used for puppies that are too young to walk around the house unsupervised or are being toilet trained. Rabbit owners have adopted these as an alternative to cage housing. Crates offer a bit more room than a cage and a lot more height than a cage, however, they do not offer as much space as a pen might.

Here are some suggestions that you can apply to a dog crate:

- When choosing a crate, choose the largest one you can afford.
- Dog crates come with no base or a tray base that is insufficient to hold mess in. It is possible to build a tray with wood or corrugated plastic.
- Dog crates have a lot of height so it's a good idea to take advantage of that by building shelves.
- If you are unable to make another level, using cardboard boxes will give your rabbits something to jump on.

- Placing lino or carpet on the base would make it more comfortable. If your bunny is messy, lino would make it easier to clean.

Dog crates can be slightly safer than an exercise pen if you have cats and dogs as it has a roof. However, predators may still be able to stick their paws in. This method of housing does not easily allow for expansion as it is made to a set size. However, if you are unable to make a cube house or use an exercise pen and cages are too expensive, a dog crate can be a good simple choice. It is even better if you are able to add extra levels to keep your pet interested. Dog crates are easily transported which means if you ever need to move, it will be easy to fold it up and take with you.

(Rabbit cage)

Free Ranging Rabbits

Some lucky bunnies have the luxury to free range within the home. This basically means that parts of the house or all of it are accessible to your pet at all times. They have the freedom to go where they wish and this is the ultimate lifestyle for a house rabbit. However, you will need to bunny proof your house. To do a room or two is not so tough but when you think about all the wires you have in your house, then you realise there's a lot that needs rearranging. Rabbit proofing is an on-going process as rabbits are quite the thinkers, when you believe you have rabbit proofed effectively, your pet will find some other way to chew that wire.

Train your rabbit into using a litter tray

If you decide to have free ranging bunnies, you might want to start with something small like a dog crate or a small pen to train your rabbit into using a litter tray. You will still need to provide a space that your bunny can call its own. Your rabbit will appreciate somewhere to hide when scared, somewhere to sleep and somewhere it can rearrange as it pleases. You can leave a crate, cage or pen open at all times and that can be your bunny's space or you can even make use of a cat basket or carry case as a place to hide. The biggest advantage of this method is that your rabbit will be happier and you will see this in its actions. Rabbits love to interact and are naturally nosy, you will find that your rabbit will follow you around the house and try and join in with what you are doing. You will witness a lot more of your pet's behaviours if you let it free range. If free ranging is something you cannot do, then please give your rabbits an appropriate amount of play time.

Chapter 4: The necessary equipment you need for your rabbits

By now, you would have made some important decisions regarding your future rabbit, such as where the bunny will live, whether you intend to adopt or buy a rabbit and how many you intend to keep. But before you can bring a bunny or two home, it is a good idea to have all the necessary equipment prepared. Here is a checklist of the things you really ought to have and what they are for.

Cage/ Hutch/ Housing – by now you've probably sorted this one out but I've placed it here all the same. If not, read the Indoor Rabbit Housing in the last chapter for details.

Water bottle/ bowl – to provide water for your rabbit. Which one works is really personal preference. I have one rabbit who insists on drinking out of a bowl and another who does not really mind. Just be aware that a bowl can spill.

Food bowls – you can have two of these, one for rabbit food pellets and the other for fresh food. Of course, you can choose not to use a bowl and hide your bunny's food in its hay. This makes your rabbit actively work for its food. However, I like to have a bowl or two just in case. Heavy bowls are better as plastic ones tend to be thrown around a lot.

Hay rack – to keep hay off the floor. These can either be placed inside or hung outside of a cage or hutch to preserve space.

Litter tray – rabbits are litter trainable so I urge you to get a litter tray. A small cat's tray works although you can also get corner trays but those are a bit small. I suggest a tray big enough for your rabbit to sit in. Some people use washing up bowls as those have sides high enough to prevent flicking of litter everywhere.

Litter – this is to use with the litter tray. There are many different types of litter available but you must make sure that the type you use is safe if ingested. Bunnies will probably have a nibble of the litter so it cannot be clumping litter that cats use. Wood or paper base cat litter can be used and there is also litter designed for rabbits.

Hay – this is something that you must have at the beginning, even if you do not have litter trays or food bowls, you must ensure you have plenty of hay. This will be your rabbit's staple diet.

Rabbit pellets – this is the concentrated feed you will give your rabbits to ensure they have the right amount of nutrients. You will only be giving your pet a limited amount of this type of feed per day as too much rabbit pellets would be unhealthy.

Rabbit Carry Case – cat basket will also do. This will be useful in transporting your rabbit to the vets. It is also a good idea to bring this with you to pick up your pet from wherever you are getting the bunny from. Pet shops usually put rabbits in flimsy cardboard boxes and some places require you to bring something to transport your rabbit in. Using a case like this means you are less likely to lose your bunny before you've even brought it home!

Other Rabbit Accessories

This second list contains equipment and items that are not immediately necessary but it would be a good idea to have these items in the future. You do not have to buy everything in one go, you can slowly add things from this list to your collection.

Rabbit toys – the best part of having a rabbit is watching them play. There are a large number of toys available on the market, plastic toys, willow toys etc. You can also make toys for your rabbit to play with using simple things like the cardboard toilet roll and unwanted boxes. There are toys they can throw, toys they can chew and toys they can push. You need not use rabbit toys only, if you look in the cat toy section, you will come across some hard plastic toys. Some places do a cheap bag of plastic toys for a pound and you get around 4-5 small toys. My rabbits love to throw and push these around. If you do use plastic toys, please make sure it is hard plastic as you do not want them eating it.

Grooming brushes – this is more of a concern if your rabbits have medium to long hair. They would need brushing fairly regularly to prevent knots. You will still need a brush for short hair rabbits but you may only need to brush them every few days and more often if they are moulting. There are brushes designed for rabbits although cat brushes can also be used. Combs will help reduce knots and a slicker brush will remove dead hair. I make use of a slicker brush when my rabbits are moulting. If you are using a slicker brush made for cats (and some of those made for rabbits), you will notice that the metal ends can be a bit scratchy so do not use a lot of pressure when brushing your rabbit as you do not want to scrape their skin off instead! I also own a massage brush made of rubber. It massages my rabbits and dead hair sticks to it too which is a bonus. I like to use it after the slicker brush. Because it is made of rubber, I tend not to keep it where rabbits can reach as they like to bite it.

Panacur Worming paste – you can buy this from veterinary clinics and some pet stores. Rabbits can have parasites called Encephalitozoon Cuniculi (E. Cuniculi). This is a parasite that lives in the cells of animals, not just rabbits. A human who is immune-compromised may run the risk of being infected. Understanding E. Cuniculi and Panacur can be rather confusing at times but this is the gist of it:

- Rabbits can be carriers of E. Cuniculi without any outward symptoms. It is when the parasite reproduces that symptoms may occur, such as head tilt, paralysis, incontinence, cataracts and renal failure.
- Parasites that reach the kidney can spread through the urine as spores and these can be released in the urine for up to 3 months. The spores can then survive in the environment for a month. This means any other rabbit living or using the same area as an infected rabbit can become infected too. Mothers who are carriers can also give their babies the parasite through the placenta. E. Cuniculi can also travel through the blood to reach the brain and cause neural symptoms to emerge.
- Panacur is a type of preventative treatment to help control E. Cuniculi which many vets claim to be prevalent across the whole of the UK. It contains a type of medicine called Fenbendazole. Panacur states that there is a wide safety margin when using this on

71

rabbits, which means your rabbit, is unlikely to gain a reaction from taking the wormer.

- It is recommended that a 9 day dose of Panacur is sufficient to prevent E. Cuniculi when used twice yearly or when they move to a new home or are about to get neutered.
- If the rabbit is displaying symptoms of E. Cuniculi or has been diagnosed with it, Panacur recommends a 28 day treatment however many experienced rabbit owners claim a 6 week treatment is more effective. Be sure to consult a vet before treatment as I am not experienced in animal medicine so cannot make any claims.

While you do not need this straightaway, I would put it quite high up on the priority list as the parasite can seriously hinder a rabbit's lifestyle.

Flystrike Protector Spray – Flystrike is a condition caused by flies laying eggs on a rabbit. The maggots will eat the rabbit's flesh and if not treated, will lead to a rabbit's death. This is a very serious condition as hot weather and unclean hutches tend to attract flies. Bunnies with dirty bottoms are more likely to have this problem. You can protect your rabbit from flystrike by using a spray. Many pet shops sell this kind of spray. I use Johnson's Flystrike Protector. I have not tried any other so cannot make a recommendation but so far I have not found any problems with this one. Always ask a vet if unsure but it is definitely a good idea to use a spray during the summer months. Some sprays also help against fleas.

Microwaveable Heat Pad – if your rabbits live outdoors or the house is particularly cold, then you can purchase a heat pad. Do not use water bottles as they may chew through the rubber and scald themselves. Always follow instructions carefully as the heat pad will be quite hot when heated. You should not use it with ill rabbits, rabbits with trouble moving and in cramped conditions as your bunny will need to be able to move away if they are too warm. The heat pad should not be a plugged in one in case your rabbit chews through a wire. The SnuggleSafe Microwavable heat pad is an ideal choice as it has no wires; it's a hard material that is safe from chewing, contains a fleece cover and is used by many rabbit (and pet) owners.

Ice Pack for Hot Weather – there are products available on the market that you pop in the freezer and when it's hot you can pop it in the hutch or cage. Rabbits can become too hot and suffer from heat stroke so it's a good idea to have something in the freezer ready. You can buy an ice pack or you can pop some bottles of water in the freezer and when those have frozen, you can pop that in the hutch/cage. I have only used this method and have found that condensation does make a mess in the cage but that is easily mopped up. As I have not used a particular product, I cannot say if they work better or not.

Nail Clippers – rabbit nails grow continuously and unless they are given plenty of hard surfaces to run on, they will need clipping. You will need to find a pair that feel comfortable in your hands and there is a large variety of clippers available, some work quite differently from others. You will need to clip regularly and as long as you do that, you will only need to clip a small amount at a time.

Chapter 5: How to litter train a rabbit

In a space of one year, I have tried several types of litter for my rabbits. My main concerns when finding litter was absorbability, odour control, safety, ease of use and price!

Very soon after I got my rabbits, I tried litter training them. Well, it's not so much that you teach them something but rather that you take advantage of their habits. So what I will do here is give you a quick lesson on litter 'training', talk about rabbit litter trays and then I will give you my opinions and ratings for the litter types that I have used in the past in my quest for the ultimate litter. I will also include information on other types of litter that I have not used and a link to the sites I gained that information from, if you wish for further reading.

Spot that rabbit corner

If you were not aware that rabbits will use a litter tray, then you may have noticed that your rabbits used **one corner** of their home as a main toilet area. Litter training is simply finding the corner your pet likes to urinate on the most and sticking a tray there with some of their droppings and wet litter. It really is that simple. You will find that at the beginning, they may occasionally use other areas but will mainly urinate in the corner with the tray. They will still leave droppings in many areas but large clusters will hopefully be in the tray. Just pick up the stray droppings and throw them back in the tray.

Word of warning, if you have not neutered/spayed your pet, they may leave a large amount of droppings scattered around. This is a mark of territory and is done by wild rabbits. A week after I had my boys neutered, they were using the tray 99% of the time for droppings. When I let them out to play, they will always run back to their litter trays to do their business. Even when I took them to visit my sister's cats (yes, cats! My rabbits are the same size as my sister's cats and they get on really well!) and I placed a litter tray they had used before in the hall way, they would still make their way back to the tray. Rabbits really are clean animals when given the chance to be.

Training free ranged rabbits

If you have free ranging house rabbits then I would suggest you confine them to one room till they are used to using a tray and slowly build on the number of rooms they have access to. You will probably have to buy several trays to put around the house at first which you can slowly reduce till you know which tray they will use. If they forget to use the tray (when I mean forget, I mean a large cluster of droppings or urine, not a stray dropping) then reduce the number of rooms they have access to. Before you know it, you will have no mess!

Cleaning the litter tray

It is easy to clean a tray, use a litter scoop (cat trays and cat scoops work fine in this regard) that has gaps big enough to let litter through but not so big that the droppings go through too. With some sifting action, you will be able to get rid of most droppings without wasting litter, but be sure to scoop wet litter out first! This works really well for my bigger rabbit

Summer but Nibbles the Dutch bunny has very small droppings in comparison. Instead of sifting, I push all litter and droppings to one end of the tray (after removal of wet litter) and I tilt the tray slightly so droppings roll to the other side of the tray. I keep shoving the litter around so droppings will roll down. It's impossible to get every dropping but it's the best method I have at the moment since the litter and the droppings are the same size and no scoop will work. These methods works for my old litter (Back 2 Nature) and may not work so effectively with other types. With Megazorb, which I am using now, I just scoop out the areas with loads of droppings.

How to choose a good rabbit litter tray:

There is a variety of small animal litter trays available on the market nowadays. Some are corner trays, made to use less space in a cage or hutch. Varieties include litter trays with high backs to prevent rabbits from urinating over the top – rabbits often urinate with their tail held high and this can sometimes cause them to urinate out of the tray. A cheap alternative to high backed trays is a washing up bowl. These are generally big enough for a medium sized rabbit and if you have a giant breed, you can look at storage boxes. Others come with hoods so if your bunny likes to play with litter or flick it around; the hood will keep the mess contained. Cat litter trays can be used for rabbits; they come in a variety of sizes so just pick one that will fit your bunny comfortably. My rabbits like to sleep in their tray so I picked a cat litter tray, standard size. We did start with a corner tray but that got rejected. I did not pick a high backed tray as when my buns sleep in their trays, they like to place their heads on the edge of the tray. This is all personal preference, so work out what your rabbit will use. It is easier to find something your bun is comfortable with than to force them to use something they don't want to.

Rabbit Litter Types Review

Litter types (given in the order I tried them, with ratings!). Please bear in mind that the information provided below is based on my own experiences and you may find that what worked well for me might not for you and vice versa. Sample a few to find your favourite:

Straw:

I had a nice packet of straw bedding. This was before I used a litter tray but I had heard that some rabbit owners line their cages with straw. Straw is quite safe for rabbits as they can eat it (even if it has little nutritional value, it helps teeth wear down) but after two days of cleaning the corner of the cage that was being used, I quickly switched to the wood shavings.

- *Absorbability*: 1/5 – dripping wet straw and many cloths to absorb urine.
- *Odour Control*: 2/5 – Straw does not smell bad to begin with but with some urine, it does not smell very good either.
- *Safety*: 5/5 – does no harm to your rabbit if ingested.
- *Ease of Use*: 1/5 – cleaning is quite annoying as you have to pick the clump of wet straw and then wipe up the excess liquid.
- *Price*: 4/5 – Straw is not too expensive and Pets At Home do a double compressed bag that lasts quite

long without taking so much space.

Wood Shavings:

Actually I did not intend to use wood shavings but after the straw disaster, I grabbed some of my hamster's wood shavings and shoved it in a 'corner' style litter tray. They did not readily take to using that so I got a cat's litter tray which they did use. Never use scented shavings. They may smell pleasant to our noses but it is too strong and perfumed for any pet's sensitive noses!

- *Absorbability*: 2/5 – shavings do not 'soak' up urine very well as the liquid tends to just spread. However, you are not left with dripping liquid.
- *Odour Control*: 2/5 – Does not really control odour.
- *Safety*: 4/5 – I've never notice my rabbits eating this however, depending on how good the quality of the wood shavings is, be careful of sharp bits as I once received a splinter from handling wood shavings.
- *Ease of Use*: 2/5 – easier to clear up wet patches than straw as you get less dripping.
- *Price*: 4/5 – big bags of wood shavings can cost quite cheap in some pet stores but because of the poor absorbency, you may find yourself using more shavings.

Megazorb:

Instead of floundering around aimlessly, I looked online and came across something called Megazorb. This is a wood pulp based litter that had been dried at a high temperature to destroy spores and bacteria. It claimed to absorb ten times as much as straw, to have great odour control, to be economical and as a bonus, it was fully biodegradable. This was originally designed for horses so it comes in big bags of 85 litres that look like they can last a good few months. Some rabbit owners swear by this stuff so I ordered a bag to try.

- *Absorbability*: 4/5 – This absorbed most of the urine but left the top quite wet.
- *Odour Control*: 1/5 – for some reason, my bag smelt worse than my rabbit's urine. I am not sure if it's a batch problem or just the way Megazorb is. At any rate, it was smelly enough to attract a number of small flies into the bin.
- *Safety*: 5/5 – My bunnies occasionally took a nibble but I never noticed any ill effects.
- *Ease of Use*: 4/5 – Easy to scoop up wet areas and since it was a big bag at a good price, I was not afraid to use more. However, because you cannot use a cat pooper scooper to 'sift' droppings out, I wore gloves and picked it out.
- *Price*: 5/5 – possibly the cheapest litter per litre you will ever find. Between £7-10 for 85 litres.

I used this for a few weeks before the smell and the little fly that would fly out of the bin every time I put something in the bin, unnerved me.

I stopped using this for a while but now I am back to using it. My current batches do not smell as bad as the first one and even though the smell is not as good as Back2Nature, the cheapness of it meant that I am using this one again.

Carefresh:

It seems that I always turned to my hamster in times of urgency. When Megazorb finally drove me over the edge, I grabbed my hamster's bag of Carefresh (I used to put carefresh in the corner where he went to the toilet and use wood shavings elsewhere, as wood shavings would stick to the plastic and stain the cage when wet with hamster urine) and added it to the Megazorb litter. I never tried using just Carefresh as it was so pricey to use that way since I spot cleaned the tray twice a day. I would use a small handful in the corners of the tray that were frequently showered with rabbit urine and the rest of the tray was filled with Megazorb. In a way, this reduced odours.

- *Absorbability*: 4/5 – Did a little better than Megazorb but surface would still be slightly wet so I could not give it a 5.
- *Odour Control*: 5/5 – It seemed to work well in this respect, I did not smell anything bad from the Carefresh however my opinion could be biased since I could still smell the Megazorb at that time.

- *Safety*: 5/5 – since it's made of wood pulp like Megazorb, I cannot see anything wrong with it in terms of safety. I hear it makes great bedding material.
- *Ease of Use*: 4/5 – same limitations at Megazorb but easy enough to remove from the litter tray. I liked that Carefresh came in several colours and I used the white one as it allowed me to easily spot which areas were soiled.
- *Price*: 2/5 – it felt very expensive to me even though the price range per litre you get is similar to litters like Yesterday News and Back 2 Nature. This may be due to the fact that they say its 14 litres compressed down to 6 litres. As Carefresh is quite 'airy', you end up using a bit more of it so this 14 litres turn 6 seems to run out very quick, even if I am only using it in corners.

Yesterday's News:

I used the rabbit version after I finished my bag of Carefresh but they no longer produce that one since it was the same as their cat litter. Both were the same anyway. This is a paper based litter that is made from recycled paper. The litter comes in the form of hard pellets however they now have a softer range that I am not very familiar with as that was not available when I tried this litter. Since my rabbits enjoy sleeping in their trays, I would have used the softer range if I was still using this brand of litter. I really liked this litter until I discovered a few problems with it.

- *Absorbability*: 4/5 – absorbs pretty well and the pellets keep their shape so cleaning is quite easy. However, because the pellets are quite hard, when my rabbits urinated, it would take a minute to absorb the urine. This means that unless you want your bunnies to get wet feet, you will need to put a thick layer of the litter so the liquid could seep through and get absorbed by the bottom bits.
- *Odour Control*: 3/5 – doesn't actively mask smell but smell is not too strong once urine is absorbed.
- *Safety*: 1/5 – for my bunnies that like to eat their litter, I would not recommend this litter based on my own experience with occasional bags. I believe it is made for cats therefore were not made with rabbits in mind. If you do use it, do check your trays when refilling or put a grid on top to prevent your rabbits from having access to the litter.
- *Ease of Use*: 5/5 – you can spot straight away which parts are soiled and which are not. It is possible to use a litter scoop with the right size holes and sort the droppings out of the tray via a sifting motion.
- *Price*: 3/5 – a bag felt like it lasted longer than Carefresh but you would find yourself using a bit more to stop wet feet.

Back 2 Nature

After being really upset with Yesterday's News, I turned to Back 2 Nature. Maybe I am just picky but at this point, I was feeling pretty sure that I would never find a litter to stick to. I bought a small bag of Back 2 Nature to try and was surprised to find something that works and is safe. This litter is advertised as >99% recycled paper with no additives and chemicals. The litter is soft pellets. Not as soft as Carefresh but makes quite a nice bed to lie on for your pet.

- **Absorbability**: 5/5 – absorbs liquids straight away whilst retaining its shape. Pellets do get soggy though, but that's to be expected. I only put a small heap in the corners where my bunnies do their business , as I clean the tray everyday and refill it when needed, and the surface only starts to look wet after the rabbit has gone several times.
- **Odour Control**: 4/5 – it does alright in this sector. No strong nasty smells when I am using it. The only time when its odour control capabilities fail is when the bin with used litter is almost full. Still, it does not attract flies the way Megazorb did for me.
- **Safety**: 5/5 – So far I've found coloured paper but not plastic or metal. I am really please with that as I do not worry if my rabbits eat a bit of the litter anymore.
- **Ease of Use**: 5/5 – soiled areas are darker so easy to spot. Droppings are sift-able using technique outlined in the litter training section.
- **Price**: 3/5 – I've worked out I use approximately a 30litre bag per month with 2 trays to fill. This is more expensive than some of the other ones I've used in the past but since it does what I need it to and it's not the priciest one, I am happy to keep using it.

For the time being, my search has ended there however, there are several other litter types I have heard of that has caught my interest.

SmartBedz

This is made from straw and is sold as bedding and litter. I first encountered this litter at the London Pet Show 2012 but they've been making litter for some time now. It is advertised to be super absorbent, odour binding, low dust and bio-degradable. The straw has been pulverized into pellets so there should not be any sharp pieces. I am quite keen to try this one out as I was quite impressed with their store demonstration at the London Pet Show.

Website: http://www.smartbedz.co.uk

Bio-catolet

Another paper based litter made for cats but adopted by many bunny owners. This one boasts to absorb 250% of its weight and is also bio-degradable.

Website: http://www.biocatolet.co.uk

Chapter 6: How to rabbit proof your home

Bunny proofing is essential for both the safety of your bunnies and for the safety of your home. It's a time consuming process and you will find that it is also an on-going process. It will be necessary to review and possibly change the way you bunny proof over time. For instance, when I first got my bunnies and they were living in the dining room, I could put anything on the dining room table as they could not reach it. But now, at one years old, they can jump pretty high so I've had to re-evaluate where things are placed. The table is no longer safe to place high risk items.

By high risk items, I mean things like:

- Electric cables
- Plants that are potentially poisonous or plants you do not want grazed on
- Anything that contains liquid that you would not want all over the place
- Cutlery or sharp objects such as scissors

If you consider how many cables you have around your house, you can begin to see the enormity of the task. However, do not feel put off! If your rabbits live in the house, you should always start by just proofing the room they are in and slowly working out towards other rooms you wish them to have access to. Starting out with just one room is a good idea in many ways, it allows your bunnies to explore the room and become familiar with it so when they are finally allowed in other parts of the house, they will view that room as theirs and see it as a safe base from which they can begin their explorations. It also means you can litter train them in a confined area whilst you prepare the rest of the house.

In this chapter, I will describe some ways you can bunny proof your home. There are plenty of other ways and with some creativity; you might come across some unique ideas (which I hope you would share with fellow rabbit owners!). You will need to remember that not all methods will work with your rabbits and that some methods might stop working in the future. You know your rabbit best so you will have to try and out think them. Good luck and play safe!

Electric Cables

Rabbits are natural chewers and because of that, they are at risk to being electrocuted in home environments. For their safety and yours, it is essential to keep them away from wires. You cannot presume that by watching your rabbit closely, no accidents will happen. It only takes a few seconds for a rabbit to chew into a wire. I will list some ideas for preventing shocks.

The area where your TV is will have an immense number of cables, particularly if you have things like digital TV boxes, game consoles etc. My advice will be to block that whole area off. A million wires hanging around, it's like an accident waiting to happen. You can cover each individual wire but if you have as many wires as I do, it would be easier, more cost effective just to impose a bunny ban in that area. You can use pet pens to block off access. If you are handy at cutting mesh, you can make a perfect mesh cover for those gaps that a rabbit can squeeze in to attack cables. Another option is to make use of hard plastic like Perspex sheets. These are quite nice as you can get see through ones that do not impair the look of your TV area as much as a play pen might. I use cardboard to cover up my TV area when I let my rabbits out as I live in my parents' house and they would not appreciate me changing the layout of the room. Luckily, mine are not crazy about cardboard so they rarely attack it.

For standalone wires, such as your phone charger or laptop charger, you can cover these wires with hard plastic. Some options are:

- **Plastic tubing** – you can buy plastic tubing (mainly the transparent kind you see in fish tanks although there are black ones available) and make a slit all the way down the tubing so you can slot your wire into it. You can also buy some that are already slit down the middle. Ensure the tubing goes all the way along the length of the wire. If needed, use strong tape to secure the tube shut at intervals.
- **Spiral cable wrap** – these are sold as cable tidies but you can use it to protect cables from those strong teeth. You can find them in most hardware stores.

You can also run cables behind furniture such as sofas and beds etc. provided that your rabbit can not reach those areas. Please make sure you do not create a fire risk though!

Wallpapered walls

Rabbits just love tearing bits of paper. Why buy a paper shredder when you can have a rabbit? Sometimes they love shredding so much, they will target your walls. It doesn't take a lot, just a little bit sticking out is enough to attract their attention. To protect your walls from destruction, you can place plastic sheets over the wall. You can find clear ones and you do not have to cover the whole section of the wall. The bottom feet or two should be enough to prevent them finding something to tear at. You can cover sections with furniture too. Placing toys or distractions where there is a chance of rabbit destruction may also be an effective method.

Skirting boards

These wooden bits that stick out of a wall appeal to rabbits. Mine just cannot resist taking a chunk out of the board. You can use wooden boards to place over a skirting board so your bunny can bite on that instead. Some chewing deterrent sprays may be helpful when sprayed on skirting boards and other areas you do not want to have chewed. Just be sure to make sure it is safe for the rabbit and safe for the furniture. It should be noted that your rabbit might actually like the spray you use so you may have to trial and error if you wish to use a spray.

Training your rabbit to leave those areas alone is also possible. You can use a water mist spray but this is only effective if you catch them every time. You can also use a word to signify that you do not like what they are doing. For my rabbits, I say 'No' in a firm voice that is reserved for naughty buns only. They seem to recognise this to some extent and will usually stop what they are doing. Never shout, always tell them in a firm way and never hit your pet.

Curtains

If you have floor length curtains, your rabbit may see them as an interesting place to hide behind. Your rabbit might also think that your curtains are lacking exits. And consequently create some. The only effective method would be to take up your curtains so they no longer trail on the ground or to make use of shorter curtains. Another method is to provide distraction toys.

House plants

House plants have to be out of reach. Placing them on a table may not be good enough as rabbits have strong legs and can reach heights that you would not have imagined. House plants can be very toxic and the best thing you can do is to put your house plants in a room that your rabbits are not allowed in. Play pens can be used to block of areas of the room with a plant in it. Be sure to check if your rabbit can reach fallen leaves or flowers as these may also be toxic.

Furniture

If you have sofas or beds that are raised, you will have to watch out for bunnies that burrow underneath and into the soft fabric. To prevent that from happening, you can use cardboard to block off these areas that your rabbit might crawl under. Even crawl spaces between a wall and a long sofa can be problematic. Rabbits can chew into a sofa and hide inside or they can become squashed between a sofa and a wall. Block off access to these crawl spaces.

Do not leave any items that can be dangerous on sofas and beds as rabbits are able to jump onto these surfaces. Rabbits can be rather clumsy so try not to put things like magazines or loose cushions on leather or slippery surfaces as they are likely to jump on and slide back off (maybe due to the fact that they have furry feet and no rubber paws like cats and dogs). Sharp objects, hot drinks or food should all be placed out of a rabbits jumping reach.

If you have furniture that moves like reclining armchairs, be mindful of how and when you use them as your rabbit may get trapped or hurt. It's best to not use the mechanisms if a rabbit is out and about. This applies to rocking chairs too.

Use a chew preventing spray if your rabbit enjoys destroying your furniture or offer them toys that are more interesting.

Bathroom or kitchen

I recommend not letting your rabbit into the bathroom if you keep all your cleaning products in there as they may become curious and play around with these chemicals. It is also a good idea to block access to this room as a bunny can easily jump into a toilet or into the bathtub. Bathtubs are slippery places and rabbits will jump in regardless of what's on the other side. They may even try to balance on the bathtub ledge and that can be disastrous if they slip and fall off.

The kitchen can be fine if they have no way of reaching counter surfaces where you may keep glasses, knifes etc. But you will have to keep the floor spotless as rabbits do not always know what is good for them. Do not let them in the kitchen whilst cooking in case you trip over your rabbit and your dinner flies across the room. Cooking fumes are probably not too healthy for a rabbit's delicate lungs. If you feel that it will be difficult to keep the kitchen a hazard free and clean environment, then I would advise you place a baby gate in front of the door or keep the door shut when your rabbits are out.

Adequate Distractions

By providing toys, you can reduce the chances of your rabbit destroying your house. Toys need not be expensive; they can be made from household items like tissue rolls stuffed with hay. If you have an apple tree, twigs from that can make nice distractions. Willow toys and cardboard castles can make fun toys for your pet. You can buy cardboard castles or better yet, you can recycle any boxes you have and make a castle.

If you place these toys in areas that are at risk of being chewed, your rabbit might attack these toys instead. You will need to swap toys around to keep your pet interested. I like to put all my rabbit toys in a box and choose a few to place out, swapping them around every few days. If you do notice your rabbit ignoring the toys you have up, try swapping them as they might be bored with those toys or they might not like those toys.

Bunny proofing may seem like a tedious task that requires a lot of thinking like a rabbit and rearranging things. If something looks dangerous, it probably is. Everything will need to be assessed and then assessed some more. However, your rabbit will thank you for it as they will be given a safe environment where they can binky to their heart's content.

Chapter 7: Rabbit outdoor housing – hutches, sheds or garages

By now, you ought to have some idea of whether your rabbits will be living outside or inside. If you have decided on outdoor housing, here are some pros and cons of each type of housing.

Rabbit Hutches

This is the traditional housing method for rabbits. A hutch is basically a wooden structure with weatherproof roofing. They come in various sizes and shapes although generic ones are rectangular with either one floor or two. Hutches will have a smaller area which is shielded so the rabbit can hide and a larger area which will have strong mesh so you can see your pet and your pet can see its surroundings. Both sides will be fully accessible with doors. Firstly, I will go over the basic things to look out for in a hutch, then I will talk about the various styles and finally I will give you some pros and cons of using a hutch and where to position it.

Make sure your rabbit is safe

When choosing a hutch (or making one, if you feel daring) it is important to ensure that it is rabbit safe. There may be many cheap hutches available but those could be poorly made or use materials that are not good for rabbits. A poorly made hutch will not be very durable and in the long run, you will find yourself replacing it. If you consider the possibility that some rabbits live up to ten years, it is in your best interest to choose something that lasts, even if it means paying a bit extra for quality.

A good hutch will have roofing felt. This will prevent water from leaking into the hutch. Roof should be slightly slanted towards the back so water does not drip in through the mesh at the front.

The wood used should not be toxic as rabbits may chew on it and the outside should be painted with non-toxic wood preservative. If the hutch is not painted with protective preservative, you can easily find some of this paint in any DIY store. By applying a few coats and reapplying every year, you ensure that you get the most use out of the hutch.

The mesh windows are usually made from chicken wire or weld mesh, the latter being stronger. It needs to be at a thickness that will not break if a rabbit tries to bite it or a predator tries to get in. Gaps between the wires should not be so big that a cat can fit its paw in. It should be securely attached on to prevent rabbits from pushing out or foxes from getting in.

The mechanism for keeping the door shut should at least be a bolt. This is probably one of the more important points if you live in an area with many foxes. Foxes are cunning animals that have been known to open a hutch if the locking mechanism is a rotating bar of wood. Bolts are a more difficult task for a fox and every time you lock your hutch door, always ensure you push the bolt as in as possible and pull the bolt handle down. Double check. If you are particularly worried about the foxes in your area it is advisable to find a hutch you can padlock or relocate your rabbits indoors. A padlock is also advisable if you have young children as when unsupervised they may not always shut the door properly. If your current hutch does not have a bolt, I urge you to screw one into place.

The hutch should always have a place for the rabbit to hide where it cannot see the outside and any predators will not be able to see it. Some rabbits have been known to die from fright, having a place to hide will reduce the chances of this happening.

It should be raised off the floor by a few inches to prevent water seeping in. If the hutch has no legs, you can improvise by using several bricks stacked on each other to create legs.

Double-decking Rabbit Hutch

Hutches used to be a one floor rectangular structure with one hiding place and one mesh window which took up 2/3rds of the hutch. Today, with people getting more creative and wanting more for their pets, there is a lot more choice on the market. Here are some of the creative ideas.

Hutches with more than one floor. Sloped 'stairs' allow the animal to traverse up and down to different levels. They may contain more than one hiding space. These are ideal if you place two rabbits in them as they allow them more room to roam and give them enough space so that they can avoid each other if they feel like it. Seeing rabbit hutches with two floors is common but there are some with three floors. Remember that the need for a ramp to move from one level to another means that you will not have twice the space of a single storey as the ramp causes areas of the hutch to be unusable.

Hutches that have a run joined to them allow the rabbit access to grass or extra running space at all times. The main hutch is usually raised off the floor with a ramp going to the ground level allowing access to the run. The size of the run itself will be different every time, depending on which model you are looking at. This hutch style allows your rabbit to have even more running space. However, you may have to go through extra steps to prevent a rabbit digging out or a fox digging in if it is on the lawn. Two ways to prevent this is to dig a mesh trench along the perimeter that goes a few feet down or to have a mesh base so the grass can grow through the mesh but no animal can dig in or out. Rotating of the hutch and run will prevent over grazing on one part of the lawn. With some DIY, you can attach a larger run to a hutch.

Hutches with removable bases for easier cleaning. Bases will be like trays that you can slide out to make spot cleaning easier. They aid cleaning so you do not have to stick your body into the hutch at awkward angles and depending on how it is made, it allows you to clean without opening the hutch. Personally, I believe these to be an unnecessary expense. My reason for this is that rabbits are creatures of habit and prefer to use the same area for their toileting needs. This means you can easily place a litter tray (a small cat's tray will do) into this area and rabbits will naturally go to the toilet there, limiting all waste into one litter tray. That way, your daily spot cleaning will be to pick out the waste from the litter tray instead of having to search around the hutch for droppings. Earlier I mentioned that some models allow you to clean without opening the hutch. Since rabbits need daily exercise and time out of a hutch, there should be one point of time every day where you should have access to the hutch to do whatever cleaning you need without your pet trying to join in with the cleaning.

Location, Location, Location

When positioning your hutch, choose an area where there is no direct sunlight during the hottest times of the day as rabbits are susceptible to heat stroke. Also choose a position where there is less draught or wind blowing at the hutch, particularly through the front as draught can make a rabbit ill. If weather conditions are rough where you live, consider buying a hutch cover.

My opinion on hutches is that a good quality one can provide good decent living quarters for your rabbits providing you choose the largest possible one you can afford and if you choose to house a pair of bonded rabbits. Why? Because of the nature of this type of outdoor housing, every time you visit your pet, you are exposed to the elements. This is all fine and dandy when its summer but in winter or when it's raining, you may be less likely to sit outside and play with them.

Don't make your bunny sad

There are certain things you must do every day such as provide hay, pellets and clean water but there will be some days where you will not spend as much time by the hutch or weather is too bad for them to play in a larger run and you cannot let them in the house. On those days, a larger hutch attached to a run and another rabbit for company may be the only thing that prevents your rabbit from becoming depressed, lonely, antisocial, and overweight and from taking up bad habits. Commercial hutches are also limited by height;

medium to large breeds will have some trouble standing up to full height without touching the top of the hutch. To prevent growth problems, they will need regular access to a run which allows them to stretch. Of course, if you are building the hutch yourself, the sky is your limit. If you feel that you may not be able to afford or build a spacious hutch or you cannot have a bonded pair, please consider a different method of housing as one rabbit at the end of the garden is one sad rabbit.

Converting shed or garage into a bunny home

Converting a shed or garage into a bunny living space has become a popular choice of housing. My rabbits used to live indoors until we found out that my dad was extremely allergic to the hay. We decided to use the garage as a rabbit home. We have a double garage and as one half is used for storage, I have used the other half to create a bunny space. Firstly, I will go into reasons why and general pointers in converting a garage or choosing a shed but since this is a creative choice of housing, I will only go over the necessities and common ideas. There are many tutorials online and many people have uploaded photos so feel free to do some research if this method appeals to you. The RWAF (rabbitwelfare.co.uk) has a good resource on shed conversion.

(Nibbles chilling in the garage)

Why use a shed or garage instead of a hutch

There are reasons for you and reasons for your pet. It enables you to spend time with your pets without freezing half to death in winter. I come from the south of England where winters only reach -5 degrees Celsius, which is nowhere near as cold as the northern parts. Even so, I would not like to be standing around outside and even though rabbits can handle cold temperatures reasonable well, I'd think given a choice, like me, they would prefer to be somewhere warmer.

Garages tend to be attached to the main house's electricity so you can place a radiator in there which allows you to keep warm (not directly next to the rabbits, of course). You can connect a shed to the house's electricity which will allow you to have a light bulb in there. Both options mean that if you should check on your pet when it's dark, you will not have to use a torch. I may sound superficial with these reasons but I do believe that the more comfortable you make an area for yourself, the more time you will spend in that area and the more you will enjoy being there. I spend many hours in my garage per day with my bunnies where I play with them and I also do my work in there.

The **reasons for your pet** are so that you can create a living space that will suit their needs more. There will be no height restriction that comes with a hutch and run and there should be more hopping space for the rabbit too. You will be able to personalise it and move things around to keep them interested and to prevent boredom. There will also be more space for toys!

(Summer playing with the castle in the garage)

Choosing the suitable shed for your rabbit

If you are using a shed, you will need to choose a suitable one. You can also convert an old shed. These are some points to consider:

- Sheds can be categorised by the type of cladding used. To prevent draughts and damp coming in, the cladding should be tongue and groove or shiplap as these interlock. Overlap cladding is cheaper but not so good for the bunny. Cladding also needs to be thick enough for rabbits to not chew through.

- The shed will need a bolt and I recommend you to add a padlock to prevent intruders from attempting to enter your shed.
- Like a hutch, it will also need protecting with wood preservative (use a pet safe one).
- Consider attaching a mesh door/screen so that you can leave the shed open for daylight and ventilation if there are no windows.
- Lino to cover the floor would protect the shed from water spillages.

When using a garage or shed, you will have to bunny proof the area. Any wires will have to be placed out of reach. One idea in a large garage is use several runs joined together to make a rabbit area free from wires. This is what I have done as the property is my parents and they would rather I not make any permanent changes to their garage! In a shed, you can have a baby gate near the entrance and then have the wires between the entrance and the baby gate so the rabbits cannot reach it. Of course, you will have to make sure your rabbits do not jump over the gate or run.

Rabbit House Furniture

Once the area is wire free, you can design how you want the space to look. Here are some brief ideas, it need not be expensive and you can always reuse things:

- Add shelves or even use an old coffee table to provide higher spaces for rabbits to sit and jump on. This also maximise play area as they can hide underneath shelves or jump around on top.
- Making a hole on the wall leading to a run outside for extra space. This is easily achievable on a shed with basic DIY skills. Use of a cat flap will minimise draughts or rain getting in.
- Reuse cardboard boxes by giving them to your bunnies; these make cheap easy beds and hiding spaces for your rabbits.
- If there are windows that you like to keep open for ventilation, consider placing mesh on top to prevent escaping rabbits. Adding netting on this will also prevent flies from coming in to harass your bunnies.

There are many ideas out on the internet so if this method appeals to you, I encourage you to research and look at photos of people's set ups.

Pros and cons with using a shed or garage

Sheds and garages allow your pet more living space. Sheds are more expensive than a hutch but for the price you pay, you get a lot more space and bad weather is no longer an issue. Converting a garage is not expensive as long as you already own the garage! But it will require you to tidy up a bit. You will need more wood preservative to protect a shed than you would if you used a hutch. But if you used a garage, you would not need any preservative.

For a method of housing outdoors, there are not many cons for using a garage or shed. I prefer this method to using a hutch. If you only intend to keep one rabbit, I would recommend letting the bunny live indoors to prevent boredom.

Other methods

The two methods above are two most common methods but no doubt people have found other ways to house their rabbits outdoors. I will not go into detail on these other methods. Whatever you do, never decide to give your whole garden as your rabbit's home. To allow a domesticated rabbit to free range unsupervised is a dangerous thing to do as there are many predators that can kill or harass your rabbit such as foxes, seagulls, birds of prey, cats and dogs. Also there is the risk of your rabbit digging out of the garden. Wild rabbits will know to run and hide from predators but a pet rabbit given the garden to live on might not know what to do.

Chapter 8: What can rabbits eat

Even though many rabbits owners are more educated on the dietary needs of their bunnies, there is still many people who do not fully understand what the main part of a rabbits diet is.

What do rabbits eat? A question that is asked often but not always answered correctly.

The majority of a wild rabbit's diet is grass, leaves, twigs, herbs and plants. For domesticated rabbits to stay as healthy as their wild counterparts, their diet should consist mainly of hay. Some people tend to think that rabbit pellets are the main meal and hay is a type of 'bedding' or just an extra nibble. Whilst hay can be used as bedding it is also your rabbit's staple diet. I'll break this topic down into three sections: **Hay, Pellets, Fresh & Dried Produce**. Fresh grass is included in the 'Hay' section.

Hay

Like I said before, this is the staple diet. Feed your rabbit plenty of hay and you are on the right path to a healthy and happy bunny. If you have a lawn, then grass is a good alternative but when your bunny is in their hutch or cage, you should leave a large pile of hay in the cage for them to eat.

Why is hay beneficial to rabbits?

1. It is full of fibre which helps keep the intestine moving. A rabbit's intestinal system needs to be constantly moving to stay healthy. As they like to chew on various objects, hay will ensure that anything that was hard to digest will be moved along by ingesting hay.

2. The action of chewing hay is good for wearing down teeth. Many teeth problems occur from not eating enough hay. Pellets may feel harder but the way of chewing a pellet and the way of chewing a piece of hay is different so they both wear down different parts of the teeth. That's why providing only pellets is not healthy for a rabbit.

3. Having hay to eat prevents boredom. Rabbits will happily sit there for hours picking out the bits they enjoy and throwing the hay around.

4. The indigestible fibre found in hay can prevent hair from accumulating in the gut. As rabbits do not spit hair balls out like cats do, it is important that they can get rid of swallowed hair in their faeces.

What types of hay are there?

Timothy Hay

This is possibly the healthiest type of hay you can feed your rabbit. Depending on the bag of timothy hay you buy, it should be a lovely green colour or a slightly tan colour. It is easiest to store as it is less damp therefore less likely to mould. It should smell sweet and fresh and you should see quite a few seed heads and many stems and leaves. The texture of the hay is hard and provides a good texture for the wearing down of teeth. Timothy hay is a good choice for obese bunnies and for general bunnies as it has low calories, fat and protein yet is high in fibre.

There are several brands from pet stores, at the moment I use Alfalfa King Timothy Hay as I found the colour and the smell wonderful. My rabbits tend to prefer this one but I find that whilst the strands are nice and long to begin with, the last third of a pack is always dusty and full of small bits that get ignored. I have also tried Woodland's Timothy Hay with Carrot and Apple. Whilst it sounds nice to me, I'm not sure if carrot and apple are very healthy additions to hay. In my opinion, it would be better to shred some fresh carrot and mix it into hay. I would like to see one with dried dandelion or other herbs mixed in as my rabbits were not very impressed with dried apple. Excel Herbage Timothy Hay with dandelion and marigold was received well in general. You can also buy large bales of timothy hay from farmers but you will need a place to store it. Bales are cheaper than pet shop hay.

Alfalfa Hay

This is a legume hay which contains as much fibre as timothy hay. It is good for younger rabbits and lactating does, but due to its high calorie/protein/calcium content, it is unsuitable for rabbits that are over a year old. The high calcium can cause sludge in urine and the high calorie content can cause a rabbit to gain weight. It is a rich green colour with a distinct smell and many leaves.

Many rabbits enjoy this hay so I am under the impression that its tastier as given a choice, my rabbits would rather nibble on alfalfa than timothy hay. Unfortunate for them, as I do not feed them alfalfa hay anymore. They used to have a bit but I was weary of the calcium content as my rabbit also had slightly thicker urine. You can give a bit to rabbits over a year old as a treat but if they are prone to kidney stones, stay away from alfalfa. It is also a good hay to help stimulate underweight rabbits to eat.

Oat Hay

This hay has a similar nutritional analysis to timothy hay which makes it a great alternative. If your rabbits do not like timothy hay (yes! They can be so picky sometimes!) you can try oat hay as it has a completely different texture and taste. Oat hay has grain husks that many rabbits enjoy the taste of.

I've tried two types of oat hay with my rabbits. The first type I tried is Burns Green Oat Hay. My rabbits were not so keen on the coarse stems but did nibble some of the seed heads. I've tried Alfalfa King's Oat, Wheat & Barley Hay. Whilst this is not all oat hay, it has a nice variety of other hays and my rabbits enjoyed foraging for their favourite bits. Once again, I found them not too fond of stems.

Meadow Hay

This is soft yellow/green hay that smells quite sweet. It is less coarse than oat or timothy hay and can be quite stringy as the strands are very thin. It has a variety of grasses, flowers and herbs which encourages rabbits to dig through and look for their favourite bits. This type of hay contains a bit more protein and a bit less fibre than timothy hay but it is cheaper (due to being more easily grown) and appears to be tastier than timothy hay. That could be due to rabbits preferring the softness of meadow hay over timothy hay.

This is readily available in the UK unlike timothy hay which is not usually grown here due to the climate being less suitable. You can buy bales of this from local farms and big bags are available on the internet and at pet stores. I've used two brands and both were received well by the buns (Pure Pastures Meadow Hay and Devon Meadow Hay). My rabbits love meadow hay so much, if you have a bag, they will bite a hole in it to get to the hay. I use meadow hay as the main hay as they eat more of this. Even though it is not as good as timothy hay (which I still give but is not always finished), the general rule is some hay is better than no hay.

Grass Hay

This is dried grass. There are two types that are readily available, one is literally the same kind of grass you expect to find in the UK and the main brands are Readigrass and Excel Barn Grass. It has a higher protein and calcium value than other hays apart from alfalfa and the amount of fibre is not as high as the other hays. The second type is orchard grass which is nutritionally similar to timothy hay. It even looks similar to timothy hay in appearance. You can feed this freely to your rabbits whereas I would suggest giving less Readigrass if your rabbits are susceptible to kidney stones.

Buying hay from local farmers is the cheapest way to go as you can buy bales of it provided you have the storage space. However, you must keep the hay dry and let it breath to prevent damp and mould. As long as it's kept in good conditions, hay can be kept for a long time.

Fresh Grass

If you have access to fresh grass, this is an excellent alternative for hay. You can leave your rabbit in a run on your lawn (make sure it is supervised!) and let him eat grass. Or you can pull fresh grass from your lawn to give to your rabbit. You will still need hay in the cage or hutch but you might notice that the more grass your rabbit eats, the less hay you will need to give. This means a bale of hay can last a bit longer. You will need to check that your rabbit can handle fresh grass as I know some rabbits are less tolerant to it for some reason. I know too much grass and my rabbits produce too much cecal faeces (soft droppings) and that they do not eat those which can be a hygiene hazard. Any grass with no pesticides, chemicals and is not next to a busy road is safe for your rabbits.

Fresh and Dried Produce

One of the best things about having a rabbit is watching them eat their veggies. One of my most interesting experiences is feeding my rabbits coriander and mint. I fed them coriander first and I placed my face in front of their and whilst they were chewing, you can smell the coriander being crushed when they breathed. Then I fed them some mint and this time you can smell mint as they breathed out. It sounds a bit odd but just try watching them eat at a rabbit level and you will see what I mean!

Introduce new food slowly to your rabbit

There are some fresh foods that you can feed your bunny. With all new foods, you have to introduce them slowly. What I usually do is give them a small piece and monitor the litter tray. If their droppings look the same as usual, I will give them a bit more but if the droppings come out slightly softer, I would scrap that off the list of things to give my rabbits. Be aware that some foods are toxic to rabbits. Also, any fresh food you give them must be clean and not rotting.

Rabbits have delicate digesting systems

General rule is, if you won't eat it, do not expect your rabbit to as they have delicate digesting systems and food that is off will upset the balance in their stomach and intestines.

Some owners suggest giving some fresh food every day. With the rising costs of everything in UK, buying vegetables for rabbits can sometimes be quite expensive. I give mine what I find in my fridge, for instance, if I am having carrot tonight, I will cut the tops off and give them to my buns or if I am having broccoli, I will put some aside for them. By doing this, I do not end up buying lots of veg that I (and them) cannot finish, I ensure that I only give them food that is fit for human consumption and I make sure they get some fresh food regularly. I do not give them fresh foods every day but they do get some most days.

Here is a list of fresh foods that people often ask whether rabbits can eat or not. The list states the food and rabbits can eat and I have offered my bunnies before. It is by no means conclusive and if you are ever unsure, then do not give.

- **Apple** – the **SEEDS are toxic** so do not offer those to your rabbit. The fruit is sweet so give sparingly. Apple twigs are great for wearing down teeth.
- **Banana** – this is very sweet so give as treat and do not give often or in large amounts.
- **Basil** – this fragrant herb can be given to your bunnies. Mine are sometimes keen and sometimes not.
- **Blackberry leaves** – mine loves these. I've never offered the fruit as it is quite sweet so check that before you give any.

- **Blueberry** – I've only given this once as I do not always have it at home but they seemed to like it enough. Once again, this is quite sweet so feed sparingly.
- **Broccoli** – this is an old favourite among bunnies but I've heard that too much can give gas. I've given my rabbits a tablespoon sized chunk with no issues.
- **Carrot tops** – the leafy green bits that you do not usually eat are ideal for your bunnies.
- **Carrot** – whilst many images and cartoons depict rabbits holding onto a huge carrot, they are not actually eaten by wild rabbits! Wild rabbits might eat the leafy tops but they rarely dig up the whole carrot. Carrots are sweet so only offer a little bit and not too often.
- **Celery** – you can give leaves and stem. My rabbits love the leaves but are picky with the stem. Funnily enough, when I leave celery in the cages, they will turn up their nose but once I'm gone they will chomp it down anyway. Make sure pieces are not too long as the stringy bits can pose problematic.
- **Coriander** – this may be a bit strong for bunnies who've never had coriander before but I found that both my rabbits really enjoy coriander. I find the taste of coriander is a good herb to mask the taste of medicine when crushed.
- **Cucumber** – I've heard that rabbits will like this. Mine did not like cucumber at all.
- **Dandelion** – the whole plant, flowers and root is yummy for rabbits. You won't find this in the supermarket but if you have a garden, you may find it growing. If the soil it is growing in has been treated

with chemicals, do not give to your rabbit. It helps rabbits who have a problem with passing liquid.

- **Grapes** – I've only given them the seedless variety and I've given them part of the stick vine bit that the grape is attached to. They quite enjoy it. At first I was unsure whether it was safe but grape growers have complained about wild rabbits eating the vine so I figured it was safe enough. They did not have any reaction to it.
- **Lettuce** – NEVER feed ICEBERG varieties. I have given mine romaine lettuce and little gem lettuce. These are quite refreshing on a hot summer's day.
- **Marigold** – I heard these flowers are tasty for bunnies. I have not yet fed them any of this as I am in the process of trying to grow some.
- **Pak Choi** – mine love the dark leafy bits.
- **Parsley** – Another yummy herb my bunnies enjoy.
- **Peppermint** – this is the mint you can buy from the fresh herb section of supermarkets. Aside from making nice tea, it also makes nice bunny feed.
- **Rocket** – this is a type of salad leave that's quite bitter. Funnily enough, bunnies don't mind the bitterness; mine go mad for a bag of rocket.
- **Rosemary** – my rabbits turn their nose up at this but it is safe.
- **Spinach** – this is really tasty. I eat some as I feed my rabbits some but if your bunny, like my Nibbles, tends to get sludgy urine or kidney stones, feed in moderation.
- **Spring greens** – I've only bought this once to see if my rabbits liked it. They did but because we do not cook it at home, most of it went to waste.

- **Squash** – I've given mine the butternut variety before but they had little love for it.
- **Strawberry** – the leaves and fruit is fine for rabbits but do not give too much as it is quite sweet.
- **Watercress** – I usually get a bag of rocket, watercress & spinach salad. They do enjoy some watercress.

Dried produce is dried herbs. You can try drying your own in an oven at a low temperature for a few hours or in a boiler cupboard or you buy yours. Some companies do packs of mixed herbs and plants, all in one. I'll list the ones my buns have tried but like above, it is not a complete list and if you are ever worried, do not offer it. As my rabbits like all the dried stuff they've been offered, I'll leave the comments to a minimum!

Rabbits can also eat:

- **Blackberry Leaves**
- **Chamomile**
- **Chicory**
- **Coltsfoot**
- **Clover**
- **Dandelion Flower, Root and Leaves**
- **Echinacea**
- **Ginkgo**
- **Mallow**
- **Nettle**
- **Parsley Stalk**
- **Peppermint**

- **Plantain**
- **Willow Twigs**

Rabbit Pellets

There was a misconception (and there still is for those who are unaware) that rabbit food is a complete diet for bunnies. You must always provide hay and water, plenty of both. Rabbit pellet is a concentrated feed; it provides all of the nutrients a rabbit may need in a concentrated form. When you consider a wild rabbit, their diet involves eating lots and lots of grass and herbs that are low in nutrients. They will eat all day to get the amount of nutrients they need. Rabbit food is very different in that you only need to feed a little bit due to the high nutrient content.

No rabbit food on the market is a complete diet

It is meant to accompany hay, rather like a side dish.

Even though pellets are hard, they do not wear down a rabbit's teeth in the right way which is why you cannot just feed pellets alone. Most rabbit foods state on the packaging that hay should also be offered in unlimited amounts nowadays. It is possible to not feed pellets but that requires the owner to be very knowledgeable in rabbit nutrition as you will need to substitute pellets for other foods that would offer a healthy amount of nutrients.

I would not suggest you do this unless you were very confident that you can provide a good diet plan. There are two types of foods on the market, the 'luxury' kind and the 'plain' kind.

Luxury rabbit feeds are colourful and appeal to us

They contain lots of different parts such as pea flakes, seeds, dried sweetcorn etc. They look fun but they encourage selective feeding. Rabbits are able to pick out which bits are yummy to them and they leave the bits they dislike. This means they are not getting all the nutrients that are needed. Poor luxury feeds contain a lot of grains, sugars and fats which are not suitable for rabbits. A rabbit diet should consist mainly of fibrous foods and that applies for this too. If you choose to offer this kind of feed, you should check that it is high in fibre and with fewer grains. You should also ensure that your rabbit does not eat selectively. Do not put any fresh food into their bowl till all the old food is eaten. If you cannot make sure of that, then you should choose the option below.

What are pellets made of?

Plain rabbit feeds are dull green brown in colour and look rather boring. Each pellet has the same nutritional value and you do not need to worry about selective feeding. These pellets usually have hay or grass as the first ingredient. Some are made from alfalfa and these pellets contain a lot more protein. Alfalfa based pellets should only be given to young rabbits or lactating does to help them grow or produce milk. As young rabbits grow older, gradually move them onto grass/hay based pellets. Young rabbits can also be given pellets freely. As they grow older, the amount of pellets should be slowly reduced. Check the packaging to see how much you should give your rabbit per day and split it into two meals. Your rabbit does not need a lot of pellets per day so if you find your rabbit is not eating much hay, try cutting down on pellets gradually as you may be giving too much. A handful a day is sufficient so do not be afraid to give less when it comes to pellets as you really do need to get your rabbit eating the good stuff: hay.

Good quality pellet

I recommend using a good quality plain pellet food. I believe the 'luxury' stuff to be unhealthy for rabbits. Look for one high in fibre and low in sugars, protein and fats if you are buying for an adult rabbit. If you are buying for a young rabbit, look out for high fibre and high protein pellets. Do not buy many bags of pellets in one go as the amount of vitamins in the pellets reduce over time. Always make sure you know how much pellets you are giving your rabbit, grab a plastic cup, measure and mark it. It is very easy for a rabbit to gain weight but hard for them to lose it. If you are cutting down on pellets, make sure you do it gradually.

If you are unsure of what pellet food to use, I have a <u>useful</u> <u>guide</u> which tells you what to look for, the ingredients and the nutritional content of some popular brands of bunny food.

Chapter 8.2: Don't feed your rabbits these! Toxic plants and foods

There are many plants and foods that are toxic to rabbits or extremely unhealthy to the point of where they just shouldn't be offered. Most processed foods for humans will not be accepted by a rabbit's digestive system. It is not worth the risk to feed them something that you are unsure of, you may poison your rabbit and you may be faced with a huge vet bill so stick to the safe stuff and always check what you feed your bunnies. If you have young children, make sure they understand the consequences of feeding a rabbit something that is not good for them. Do not give young children the responsibility of feeding a rabbit unless they are very responsible.

The list I provide here is a few example of the common toxic food to rabbit. This list is not conclusive, just because something is not on this list does not mean it is safe.

- Almond
- Apple Seeds
- Apricot – all parts but fruit
- Asparagus Fern

- Avocado
- Buttercup Leaves
- Cardinal Flower
- Cherry tree – all parts but fruit
- Chinese Evergreen
- Chocolate
- Christmas Candle – Sap
- Christmas Rose
- Coffee bean
- Corn Plant
- Daisy
- Elderberry – unripe berries, stem and roots
- English Ivy
- European Buckthorn
- Fireweed
- Garlic
- Horse chestnut – nuts and twigs
- Hydrangea
- Indian Turnip
- Indigo
- Inkberry
- Iris
- Ivy
- Jasmine
- Mango
- MayApple
- Nutmeg
- Oak – acorns and foliage
- Onion
- Peach – leaves, twigs and seeds
- Pear – seeds
- Potato – eyes, raw shoots and green parts

- Radish
- Rhubarb – leaves
- Snowdrop
- Sweet Pea – seeds and fruit
- Tomato – leaves, vines
- Tulip – bulb
- Walnuts –hulls and green shells
- Wild Mustard
- Yew – needles, seed and berries

Bonus: How to make your own rabbit toys: Vegetable Skewers

We are now giving out this mini guide for free. Visit the link www.AnimalWhoop.com/RabbitAndMe and download the free contents. The free downloads include a step-by-step guide on how to make your own rabbit toys.

Chapter 9: Why and when you should castrate or spay your rabbit: The benefits, the risks and the cost

Unless you get your rabbit from a rescue centre, chances are, your rabbit will be able to reproduce. Put a male and a female together and you will end up with babies. Doesn't that sound cute? The problem is, babies grow and have more babies and on and on it goes. There is an abundance of abandoned rabbits in shelters so there isn't a need for more bunny babies. The solution to this would be neutering and spaying.

What is castration / spaying?

Castration is done to male rabbits. The testes of the rabbit are removed by making a cut at the scrotum. If you are a man reading this, rest assured your rabbit won't find this quite as terrifying as you would! Spaying happens to female rabbits, their reproductive tract is removed.

Why should you neuter or spay your rabbit?

Aside from not flooding shelters with unwanted rabbits, there are many benefits for neutering or spaying your rabbit. Here is a list:

1. Your rabbit will not feel stressed out by hormones that are urging him or her to reproduce. They would feel happier without these hormones.

2. Your rabbit will be more calm and easier to bond with.

3. Rabbits are happier with a companion, but they are less likely to get on if they are not neutered or spayed. If you have a male and female pairing, the male rabbit will not bother the female as much. Same sex paired rabbits will be less likely to fight. Bonding new rabbits will be easier.

(These two rabbits would not have been so friendly towards each other if they had not been neutered.)

4. Your rabbits will have a longer life span. Female rabbits that are not spay are highly at risk of developing uterine cancer. The figures are high, with 80% developing this cancer after 5 years of age. Male rabbits are less likely to have testicular cancer.

5. Litter training is more successful after neutering or spaying as your rabbit will have less need to leave territorial droppings. Urine spraying would also not occur, this can be done by both males and females but male rabbits do it more.

6. Female rabbits that have been spayed will not suffer from phantom pregnancies. A phantom pregnancy is when a rabbit thinks she is pregnant and will prepare for babies by pulling her fur out to build a nest. This can become very stressful for the rabbit and she can become aggressive as a result.

What are the risks of castration or spaying my rabbit?

There are some risks involved because it is surgery, however, castration or spaying rabbits should be routine surgery for a rabbit savvy vet. Look for a good rabbit vet to lower the chances of any complications. Ask your vet questions and if they cannot give you a good answer or they seem disinterested, then perhaps you should consider finding another vet. It is ok to ask your vet how many castration or spaying operations were done in the last year and how many had complications.

One of the main risks comes from anaesthetic. Any unhealthy rabbits or rabbits undergoing other treatment should not be castrated or spayed. Consult a good rabbit vet. A rabbit should be fed right up to the operation and it is advisable to bring along some food for them to give your pet after the operation. If a vet tells you to not let your rabbit have food, find another vet! Since rabbits cannot vomit, there is no risk of food regurgitation when under anaesthetic.

Another risk is gut problems where your rabbit's digestive system might slow down. If your rabbit refuses to eat, contact a vet straight away. Operation can also stress a rabbit. Your vet will help by giving a pain relief like metacam and if necessary, something to help stimulate the digestive system.

While there are some risks, they are fairly short term and the benefits far outweigh the risks. Provided you have a trustworthy vet with a high success rate, there will be less chance of complications.

When to castrate or spay your rabbit?

You can have your male rabbit neutered once their testicles descend. This happens around 14-16 weeks.

You can have your female rabbit spayed once she is sexually mature. This tends to be after 16 weeks but you will find that most vets recommend you wait till they are 24 weeks old as spaying is a more complicated operation and a slightly older rabbit has less risks.

It is recommended that you have your rabbit neutered or spayed before they are two years old as older rabbits may be more at risk, you might have to do a thorough health check and blood work which will increase the costs of the operation.

How much does it cost to neuter your rabbit?

This will vary from surgery to surgery. You will be looking to pay anywhere between £50-80 for this operation, bearing in mind that some surgeries will charge more than that.

Post-operation care for your neutered rabbit

Your rabbit will recover fairly quickly, although female rabbits will take slightly longer. Keep your rabbits in a warm place after surgery and ensure they have food and water available. They may be slightly stressed or upset so you should leave them alone in a quiet place but frequently checking to see if they are alright and if to monitor how much they ate. Take away toys and obstacles, place a towel in the cage and avoid picking up your rabbit. Male rabbits should be ok in 2 days and females around 5-6 days.

Ask your vet if you will need to bring your rabbit back for a check-up, who to call if there is a problem and what signs to look out for.

Most vets use surgical glue instead of stitches so you might not have to worry about your rabbit biting stitches but you will need to check the operation site daily for infection. Swelling, redness and pus may be signs of infection and will need veterinary attention.

Neutering sounds like a terrible thing but it really is a safe procedure when done by an experienced vet. Do some research, ask some questions and find a vet who cares about you rabbits. Neutering made my two boys easier to train and reduced their fighting.

Disclaimer: The information here is for education purpose only. Always seek professional veterinary advice regarding neutering or spaying your rabbits.

Chapter 10: Cutting (Clipping) rabbits nails step-by-step

A rabbit's nail grows continuously. If a rabbit is given the space to run and that space is a hard surface, the nails will be naturally worn down but in most cases, the amount of wear is not enough to counter the amount of growth. Rabbit nails will need to be checked and clipped regularly. Done properly, you will only find yourself removing a 1-2mm amount each time.

I will explain how you can go about cutting nails in this page. However, if you feel unable to do this yourself, for whatever reason, you can always pop into a veterinary clinic and book to have yours done by a nurse or vet.

Some people are able to put their rabbits onto their back and cut their nails that way. My rabbits find that extremely stressful and are liable to kick which can injure them (and me!). I have noticed that one of my rabbits can be tranced into having their nails cut quickly which has saved us a lot of time and stress. If you want to know about trancing, how to do it and the why some people don't trance their rabbits, we will talk about it in the next chapter.

You will need these items to help with rabbit nail clipping:

- A pair of rabbit nail clippers that fit comfortably in your hands. I recommend those that are made for cutting rabbit nails as the size of the blades will be more suited. Most pet shops will supply these.

- A person to help hold your rabbit still. You can manage by yourself if your rabbit is very calm. I've done mine on a table by myself before and it's tough to get the most inner nail on the hands but it is doable. Having said that, an extra person means that if your rabbit panics, you are less likely to have an accident occur.

- A towel to prevent clippings going all over the place and to prevent your rabbit biting or scratching your assistant.

- Some healthy treat to encourage them to associate nail clipping with positive thoughts.

- A tub of styptic powder or corn flour/corn starch in case you cut too deep and some tissue.

How to cut/clip you rabbit's nails

To clip a rabbit nail, you must be able to identify the 'quick' on a nail. The quick is basically the blood vessel that runs into a nail. If your rabbit has light coloured nails, you can see this as the small pink red line within the nail. On a rabbit with dark nails, you can find the quick by shining a light at the nail. The idea is that you do not cut into the quick otherwise things will get really messy. Cutting into the quick will result in some blood and an irritated bun. If that happens, remember, **NEVER panic.** Your rabbit will be just fine. Dip the nail into styptic powder or corn flour and press a tissue to it till the bleeding stops. It can happen to anyone and it might seem quite scary but as long as you stay calm, your rabbit will be fine. If in any doubt, ring up your vet.

Once you are sure you can identify the quick, you can follow these procedures:

1.   Choose a room that is brightly lit and prepare yourself before you bring your rabbit into the room. If you are using a table, place the towel on the table and put the clippers, powder and tissue close by. If you are using your assistant's lap, place the towel on their lap and once again, put your tools nearby.

2.   Bring your rabbit into the room and place the bun on the table/assistant's lap. Offer your rabbit a healthy treat to help calm the rabbit down.

3·   Have your assistant put his or her hands around the rabbit's front. You should be able to firmly (but do not apply so much pressure that you risk hurting your pet) grasp a hand and lift it up slightly. If you find this difficult, ask your assistant to lightly lift the bunny up. Your rabbit's feet should still be firmly touching the table or lap.

4·   Use one hand to hold onto your rabbit's hand and use the other hand to wield the clippers. You should be able to use the hand holding the rabbits hand to brush aside the fur so you can clearly see the nail. This can be a bit tricky at first. Rabbit hands are covered in fur, making it a tough to find a whole nail. A bit of practice makes perfect. Do not worry if you cut some fur off.

5·   Slip your rabbit's nail into the clipper. You want to leave several millimetres between the clipper and the quick. If you are worried, leave more space. When you are confident about the position of the clipper, press down hard. You will need to press hard to clip a nail as rabbits have quite strong nails. Your rabbit might try and snatch his paw back, just tried to hold the paw firmly.

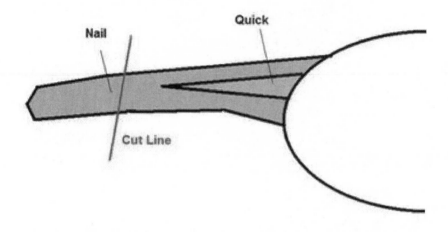

6·   Continue this for the rest of hand. There is one nail hidden on the inner side of their hands, a few centimetres up the hand, rather like a thumb nail. This will need clipping too. It might be hard to manoeuvre the clippers into a position to cut but it isn't impossible. There are a total of 5 nails. Change hands. You may find yourself physically moving to find a good clipping position. This is normal. Offer your rabbit a healthy treat if that helps and have a break if you feel you both need it.

7·   When doing the feet, there is only 4 nails and none are hidden away. Your assistant can keep their hands around the front of the rabbit. You should be able to manoeuvre the clipper in without lifting the feet up. If you do need to lift the feet up, hold the feet firmly as you do not want your rabbit to kick as you clip. Try to only lift the front part of the feet up by a bit, if you lift it too high, your rabbit may become frightened. Once again, only cut a bit; make sure you are not cutting into the quick.

8· If you do cut into the quick, dip the nail into the powder and press a tissue to it till the bleeding stops

9· Once you've done both feet, give yourself and your assistant a pat on the back and praise your bunny for being a good girl/boy!

Incorporate this routine into your monthly rabbit health check and you will only need to cut 1-2mm each time. By cutting nails, you reduce the chances of your rabbit breaking one and hurting themselves.

Chapter 11: Rabbits – To trance or to not trance

Trancing a rabbit is the act of lying your rabbit down so that he goes into a sort of trance. In such a state, a rabbit does not usually move. I never used to understand trancing because I had never managed to do it with my rabbits before. I've seen dwarf rabbits tranced on youtube before and I just thought my two were too big to be tranced. If I ever flipped them over, they would flip back. Then, out of the blue, I discovered trancing by accident.

One of my rabbits Nibbles had GI stasis over the weekend but because it was the first time he had ever had it, I was not too sure what it was. All I saw was him repeatedly lie down for a few seconds, get up and try and groom his behind and then lie down again. I had thought maybe there was something wrong with his behind, so I picked him up and turned him over. Usually, he would flip or kick but for some reason, he went slack, allowing me to quickly have a look. His behind looked fine. He went to the vets the next day and it was confirmed that he had GI stasis which fixed up after a night of hospitalisation.

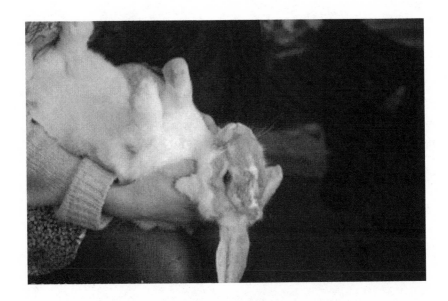

I did not really know that he had tranced that night. It was
only when we were clipping his nails yesterday that I
mentioned to my sister, who had him on her lap (I was the
clipper), that Nibbles was lying still on his back on the day he
was ill. Curious, she carefully laid him down on her legs. At
first, his head rolled back a bit and he did not move. Worried,
she supported his head. But he still didn't move. His eyes
were shut and his nose was slowly twitching. I quickly
trimmed all nails. We then did the same for Summer which
was a miracle, since nail cutting is usually a stressful activity
for Summer. What normally took fifteen to thirty minutes
(dependent on luck and mood) was reduced to five. I even

got to check their teeth for the first time. That was the first time I ever tranced a rabbit.

Trancing is one of those debates, like iphone or galaxy, mayo or ketchup with your fries. The kind where some are convinced their rabbits love it and some are so wholly against it, they refused to even look at a tranced rabbit.

The Science

Tonic Immobility or TI is what the scientists refer trancing to. It is considered to be a fear motivated defence mechanism. TI is considered a last attempt for prey to escape being eaten by a predator. When a rabbit is in a TI state, it is playing dead. There are advantages to using this method when escape seems impossible. For example, if a fox has caught a rabbit, the rabbit might play dead. Thinking its prey is dead, the fox will stop attacking and may even let go of the rabbit or loosen its grip. In a split second, the rabbit might suddenly spring to life and escape.

In a study conducted by McBride et al. the results suggested that rabbits show symptoms that are in line with being stressed after being in a TI state, such as a faster heart rate and breathing.

So...To trance or to not trance?

Some owners say their bunnies are so relaxed in this trance mode that when they wake up, they do not run off or panic but would happily sit in their owners laps. Others say that their rabbits would suddenly spring to life and are evidently stressed.

Many people would argue that it is stressful but in some cases necessary. For instance, if your bunny had an injury, needed grooming, had a dirty bum or needed nails clipped, TI can allow you to do all these things quickly. Perhaps it is stressful but most rabbits find having their nails clipped etc. stressful without TI. I suppose you could be weighing up which is the lesser of the two evils. Unless your rabbit is calm and easy going, he will probably be stressed with or without TI when you are doing any of those items. If it takes 30 minutes to clip nails without TI, you and your bunny are both frustrated, he is kicking at the same time and you are worried about cutting into the quick, perhaps TI could be useful and maybe less stressful since you could get the job done in 5 minutes.

You could always get your vet to do those tasks, but the drive to your vets can be stressful, as can being handled by a stranger at the clinic.

It's a personal thing, to trance or to not trance. I cannot justify scaring them in a car journey to go to the vets who I know will not handle them as lovingly as I do. Vets are practical and I know that one time one of my vets could not look into our rabbit's mouth so he took them into a back room where a nurse helped. I wasn't sure how much patience or care he took with checking their mouths. For all I know, he probably tranced them.

As long as owners do it responsibly and treat their rabbit with respect, I don't see why trancing cannot be used for health checks and clipping nails. I did not get kicked in the face, the nails were trimmed nicely so I can give it a bit more time before I clip again, I did not have to skip Summer's single wonky curved-in nail for fear of cutting it wrong and as an added bonus, they got their treat banana quicker because the job was done quicker.

If you do trance your bunny, do it for a good reason. It is not a party trick. Safe procedures are necessary to make sure you do not harm your bunny. Trancing should always be done close to the floor as rabbits can suddenly come of out of a trance and injure themselves. Anne Mcbride narrated a video created for Hopping Mad Bunny Magazine that is extremely useful for teaching you how to lift and handle your bunny properly. It covers how to trance safely. Look up "Handling and lifting rabbits - an expert guide" on YouTube.

Here is a bit of a mini story which makes me think that tranced rabbits are quite aware. My sister had Summer tranced on her lap as I clipped his nails and when we were done, she leant forward and kissed his nose a few times, commenting that she had never felt so close to Summer before.

The reason for that comment was because Summer and her NEVER really got on. The way how you might just not like someone, Summer was iffy towards her. So when we gently rolled him over, the first thing he did was start digging at her dress. I picked him up and he calmed down.

Conclusion? Summer must have felt violated that she had kissed him! When tranced, he had his eyes half open but he must have saw and felt something. He must have been thinking, 'I might be still but that don't make me blind!!'

Chapter 12: FIVE simple ways on how to bond with your bunny

You bring your new bunnies home and you've placed them in their new home. Then you give them time to settle. Several hours later, you come back and try to interact with them and you realise one thing. They don't seem interested in you!

That can be considered normal. Even when bonding two rabbits together, a lack of interest in one another is considered a good sign. The problem arises when they actively attack or avoid you at first sight or if after a few weeks, they still haven't warmed up to you.

Bonding with your bunny is so important because they are, for the most part, silent creatures. Dogs and cats can call for your attention but it is all too easy to forget an animal that isn't interested in you and cannot meow or bark to catch your attention. Not having a good relationship with your bunnies may mean that you might unintentionally neglect them, particularly if they are hutch bunnies.

So what I've done here is give you 5 ways on how you might increase that special bond between you and your pet. You cannot force a person to like you and it's the same with bunnies BUT you can improve your chances.

1. Take things slow when bonding with your bunny

Serious. You rush into things, you will make mistakes. Rabbits have long memories and they hold grudges. I'm not joking. If I annoy my bunnies at the start of a play time session, they are more likely to give me bunny attitude for the rest of our play time. So the first thing you must know about bonding with your bunny is that you should not rush it. Take it slowly and let your bunny choose the pace.

If you do move things along too quickly, be ready to take a step back. You may be lucky and develop a good bond within a week but it can take months and you may find that your bunny might never like being picked up etc. no matter how good your bond gets.

2. Get down on their level

To your new bunny friend, at first sight, you look scary. For all he knows, you probably want rabbit stew later, so he will play it safe. In the rabbit world, big moving things are scary. Luckily for you, rabbits may be wary but they are also curious. If you were at bunny level, your threat factor goes down and your rabbit will want to know who and what you are.

When I was bonding with my bunnies, I laid on the floor and kept very still. My bunnies left me alone for a bit but when they realised I was not going to move, they came over and started investigating. Don't be afraid if your rabbit nudges you, sniffs you or tries to climb on you, that is all part of him trying to understand you. One time I was on all fours cleaning and Summer jumped on my back for a piggy ride. When they are comfortable with your presence and scent, you can sit up. I find my bunnies still prefer it if I am closer to the floor.

3. Don't pick your bunny up

Unless you absolutely need to, don't pick the cute bunny up. I know they look like fluffy cute soft toys but when you're being kicked at, they won't look so cute anymore. Most of the time, a new bunny is not going to be impressed. You get some rabbits that enjoy being picked up but that's likely due to the trust they have for their owners. Bunnies generally disliked being picked up because to them it feels like a predator has just picked them up. A scary situation which can force you to take steps back when bonding with your bunny, trust may have to be re-established. Sometimes, you will have to pick up your rabbit, for health checks etc. but try to keep these encounters positive with soft words and treats.

4. Bond with your bunny through food

The way to a bunny's heart is with food. Rabbits are grazers and eat throughout the day. You give them food, they love you more. Try feeding their pellets on the palm of your hand.

That helps build trust. Once your rabbits are more comfortable with you, you can try holding their food by your shoulder whilst sitting on the floor. This means your bunny has to sit on you or use you as support to get to the food. I like to hold some greens or a bit of broccoli. It's also great fun to make them work harder for their food. You can also teach them their names and to come when called with the use of food. Just bear in mind not to use sugary snacks and not to overfeed your bunny.

Another method is to go down to bunny level and hold a piece of hay between your lips. My bunnies believe that if I am about to eat it, it must be nice and almost always snatch that piece of hay off me. It's a decent method of bonding with your bunny that means you can get quite close to them.

5. Speak softly

Rabbits have excellent hearing. This means no shouting, you will scare your new friend. Instead, talk to them softly. Get them used to your voice so they can associate it with being safe. You can talk to them when they are in their cage or when they are walking about.

There are probably other ways you can bond with your bunny but this is the basic five that you can begin with. As soon as your new bunny has settled in, you can begin bonding with your bunny using any of the suggestions listed here.

Chapter 12.2: FIVE steps to turn your rabbit into a happy rabbit

Not much beats watching a happy rabbit. If you have never witnessed a joyful binky (a happy rabbit will jump spontaneously, often twisting or kicking his back legs up) or a relaxed flop to one side, then you ought to make it your mission to observe your rabbit engage in happy activities. My rabbits also grind their teeth quickly and close their eyes when I rub their cheeks if they are happy. All rabbits show happiness differently but most of them exhibit the behaviours above.

Here, I will give you 5 simple steps you can take to make your rabbit happy.

Step 1: providing safety from predators

You will need to understand that rabbits are prey animals which means they can be scared of anything. A new noise or unexpected action like something falling off a table can scare or startle your rabbit so much, he runs off frightened.

Reducing fear and providing security can give way to happiness. Rabbits work out beforehand where they can hide if a predator appears. If they know they are within easy running range of a safe place, they will be more relaxed. A rabbit that feels safe will perform more happy actions like flopping.

What you can do: Provide places for your rabbit to hide. Cardboard boxes with two exit holes or long tunnels work well. Rabbits like to know they won't be cornered so by giving them two exit holes, they can always escape. If you have a house rabbit, have a hiding place in every room. If you have an outdoor rabbit, ensure there is enough places for your rabbit to bolt to when scared.

Step 2: providing exercise

Ever heard of the 'a hutch is not enough' campaign? Rabbits confined to hutches and cages for long hours will grow bored, obese and frustrated. I'm not saying that obese rabbits won't have fun, they can but being locked up all day doesn't allow for much fun and being obese shortens life span, causes more disease and ultimately shortens happiness. Wild rabbits do a lot of running and jumping every day so it follows that domesticated rabbits need exercise to keep happy. A happy rabbit will binky like no tomorrow. In a hutch, there is little room for binkying. To witness that happy behaviour, you will need to let your rabbit out to exercise and have fun.

What you can do: Easy, let them out! Outdoor rabbits can have a run. If you are busy often and want to let your rabbit have room to roam, you can attach a run to your hutch. With some careful DIY, you can make it a safe place for happy rabbits to have fun. House rabbits can be allowed out to exercise around the house when you are at home to make sure not too much trouble occurs. Otherwise, you can use play pens to make an area for your rabbit to live, which is large enough to provide exercise room for when you are not at home. Throw in some toys, rotate them often and voila! Rabbit fun will ensue.

Step 3: Feeding the right food

Rabbits are grazers. Happy rabbits get to graze all day. This might sound weird but rabbits combat boredom by eating. Sometimes I do that too. Providing good quality timothy or meadow hay is a good way to prevent boredom and increase happiness. A decent amount of veggies also puts a hop in your bunny's step. Whenever I walk in with a bowl of veg, both my boys binky and run around me. They do that too when I measure out their pellets which is why this step is called feeding the 'right' food. Pellets make rabbits happy but too much can lead to obesity and like I said earlier, that can reduce happiness in the long run. Same goes for sugary treats or fruit.

What you can do: Unlimited hay for grazing fun. Clean and safe vegetables should be given every day, look at chapter 8 on what rabbits eat to see what veg you can feed your rabbit. Reduce pellets to a reasonable amount and resist the urge to feed more when your bunny begs for it. Offer fruit and sugary treats in moderation for that little boost in happiness. Fruits are a better choice to store bought snacks. No grain treats, that is a rabbit you have, not a hamster!

Step 4: Company

Safety in numbers and the more the merrier! Living alone can be sad, especially if your owner is out all day. Rabbits can even fall in love. That is one of the best things about having rabbits. Even if your love life seems hopeless at the moment, you can at least give your rabbit the chance of finding love! Rabbits can keep each other company, groom each other and binky together.

What you can do: While rabbits like company, they can be picky about who they get. To improve your chances of finding the right match, why not give a rescue centre a go and give a rabbit a new home? Most centres allow you to bring your rabbit over and help you find a pair to match him/her to. When you see your rabbit flopped on the floor next to his or her new friend, you will feel just as happy as they do. Just make sure you follow the next step!

Step 5: Spaying and/or neutering

Instincts can be very strong and most rabbits desire to mate and pass on their genes. These instincts can be very frustrating for both domesticated rabbit and owner. Your rabbit might take part in behaviours such as spraying of urine or leaving loads of droppings outside of the litter tray. There is also a higher risk of uterine cancer in unspayed females and testicular cancer in entire males. Rabbits that got along fine when young might fight when the hormones kick in. Frustrated rabbits might hump things you would rather they did not. Lastly, you might get an unwanted litter of rabbits if you have a male and female housed together. Spaying and neutering can help relax your rabbits and help them lead a happier life so more time is spent binkying and less time is spent humping your shoe. I outlined before in chapter 9 the pros and cons of neutering and the risks involved. You will find more in-depth information there!

What you can do: Call up a vet and book an appointment as soon as your bunny is at the right age. Sooner rather than later is safer if you have more than one rabbit living together. Rabbits that fight prior to neutering or spaying have a harder to getting back together.

There you have it. I hope these steps will help your rabbit find happiness. How does your rabbit show his or her happiness? Drop me an email and let me know, I love hearing about happy rabbits!

Chapter 13: How can I prevent heat stroke and heat exhaustion in my rabbit?

Occasionally, we'll have some hot British summer weather and while it's the kind of weather most people enjoy, our rabbits might not feel the same. They can handle cold weather well, however heat stroke in rabbits can occur very easily in hot conditions.

So you may notice that your rabbit's ears are hot when stroking them. This can be a sign that your rabbit may be feeling uncomfortably hot. Overheating can be fatal if not spotted early.

Symptoms of heat stroke and heat exhaustion in rabbits:

- Do note that all rabbits differ in what temperatures they can cope with so it is up to you to keep a close eye on your pet's limits.

- Since rabbits make use of their ears to help regulate their temperature, their ears will feel hotter than usual when they are trying to cool down. They cool down by expanding the blood vessels in the ears to allow more blood through. The air cools down the blood which circulates to the rest of the body. Sometimes (not always) hot ears can be an indication of a fever.

- Overheating rabbits will be very lethargic and unresponsive.

- Rabbits that are too hot with have fast shallow breathing and may even try breathing through the mouth.

- Extreme signs of overheating will include strokes, convulsions and seizures. A rabbit at this stage may collapse in its side with unresponsive eyes. If this is happening, go to the section below to see what to do if your rabbit has heat stroke.

What can you do to prevent your rabbit from having heat stroke?

Simple answer is to not let your rabbit get to the point where he or she is too hot. Prevention is the best cause of action.

- Keep your rabbit's home out of direct sunlight. Even indoors, this is important because sunlight that enters the home through windows can be extremely warm. If some sunlight does fall on your pet's home, make sure there are adequate areas of shade. Be aware that the sun moves throughout the day so what started out as shady may become full sunlight later. This rule applies both indoor and outdoor, in hutch cage or run.

- Allow your rabbit access to clean water at all times. If your rabbit prefers bowls, I would recommend having a bottle attached for backup. In hot weather, a rabbit may drink more and water will evaporate quicker so you may need to check water levels more often. Please note that you cannot count on a rabbit to drink more water to cool themselves down when hot. To make water cooler, you can add ice cubes to it.

- Wet vegetables help increase water intake.

- I always have a few bottles of frozen water in my freezer. On hot days, I place these in their cages. I have not yet seen my rabbits lean against them but they do contribute to keeping the air cooler.

- You can place a fan in the same room. Do not aim it directly at your rabbit. Moving fans work best. Alternatively, if you have air conditioning, you can use that.

- You can place a tile in your rabbit's cage. This can be similar to the ones used in chinchilla cages. Your bunny can sit or lay on it to keep cool.

- Consider giving long hair rabbits a hair cut in summer. Help moulting rabbits brush out their old coat.

If the worst has happened and your rabbit might be going through heat stroke or overheating to dangerous levels, you will need to act fast.

Move your rabbit away from sunlight and into a shady spot. Wet a cloth with cool water. Do not use very cold water as the temperature difference may put your rabbit into further shock. Likewise, do not place your pet into a tub of water. Wipe this onto the ears, as we mentioned earlier, a rabbit's ears are his way of cooling down so the cool cloth will help lower the temperature. Maintaining this method of cooling your pet down, call your vet and ask for further instructions.

In hot weather, be careful of travelling far with your rabbit. Cars are dangerous places as they can heat up quite fast. Also, older rabbits or less healthy ones will be at more risk of overheating.

Chapter 13.3: THREE quick tips to prevent heat stroke and heat exhaustion

In a hot British Summer, we've had temperatures in the low 30s and high 20s. So what does that mean for our pet rabbits? **Deadly heat**. Pet rabbits can suffer really badly in temperatures this high. Wild rabbits have the option of hiding underground where they are surrounded by cool earth till the sun comes up but pet rabbits are stuck where they are left. So if you were not careful about the positioning of a run or hutch, or you haven't considered offering shelter, your pet might be in serious danger of heat stroke or heat exhaustion.

Just briefly though, ensure your rabbit is not lying lifeless and unable to move. Rabbits will be less responsive during the day but they should not be so unresponsive that you will find it unusual.

Here are three quick tips to keep that heat stroke and heat exhaustion at bay:

1. Crank out the cold veg! Rabbits do not always drink more when they are hot so it's your job to make sure they are well watered. This will liven any hot rabbit up and keep them well hydrated. Plus you have the added bonus of bonding with

your rabbit through food. To help prevent heat stroke/exhaustion today, I gave my rabbits some pak choi, rinsed in cold tap water and a bit of red pepper. They absolutely loved it!

2. Frozen bottles of water. My rabbits will lie near these, lick the condensation off and roll them around the room. Because the water is frozen solid, it will stay cold for a long amount of time. You can buy ice pods which are built especially for pets, they look a lot nicer but you can also recycle empty water bottles. Just fill up with water and pop in the fridge.

3. Heat stroke and heat exhaustion can be caused by direct sunlight so move your rabbit into the shade! Reposition that run or hutch so there is plenty of shade. The sun will move during the day so keep an eye out for that. Even if your rabbit is indoors, sunlight coming through glass will heat up a room to the point of being unbearably hot.

Heat stroke and heat exhaustion are two killers in summer and people often do not notice it till it's too late. Implement these three quick tips to help you rabbit feel more comfortable during the heat wave.

Attribution

Pic 1: Bradygnathia superior in a rabbit By Uwe Gille (Own work) [GFDL or CC BY-SA 3.0], via Wikimedia Commons

Pic 2: American Fuzzy Lop rabbit. public domain

Pic 3: By Gilberte at nl.wikipedia [GFDL, CC-BY-SA-3.0 or CC-BY-SA-2.5], from Wikimedia Commons

Pic 4: by valeehill via Flickr [CC BY-ND 2.0]

Pic 5: by hiwarz via Flickr [CC BY 2.0]

Pic 6: by coalybunny via Flickr [CC BY 2.0]

Pic 7: Netherland Dwarf By Lauri Rantala (originally posted to Flickr as Höpö) [CC-BY-2.0], via Wikimedia Commons

Pic 8: by Squish_E via Flickr [CC BY 2.0]

Pic 9 : Havana Rabbit breed By Mjm91 (Own work) [CC-BY-SA-3.0], via Wikimedia Commons

Pic 10: by katattack via Flickr [CC BY-ND 2.0]

Pic 11: by Carly & Art via Flickr [CC BY-SA 2.0]

Pic 12: Schwarzes Kleinsilber-Kaninchen By 4028mdk09 (Own work) [CC-BY-SA-3.0], via Wikimedia Commons

Pic 13: House rabbit, Standard Chinchilla breed by Xoxi at en.wikipedia [CC-BY-SA-3.0 or GFDL], from Wikimedia Commons

Pic 14: A Tan rabbit (black) owned by Kelly Flynn of Blue Ribbon Rabbitry By Kelly Flynn – Blue Ribbon Rabbitry (Own work) [GFDL, CC-BY-2.5 or CC-BY-3.0], via Wikimedia Commons

Pic 15: American Sable Rabbit By Sonofsammie at en.wikipedia [CC-BY-3.0], from Wikimedia Commons

Made in the USA
San Bernardino, CA
14 October 2018